Ever Hear of Feuerbach?

Ever Hear of Feuerbach?

*That's Why American and European Christianity
Are in Such a Funk*

MARK ELLINGSEN

 CASCADE *Books* • Eugene, Oregon

EVER HEAR OF FEUERBACH?
That's Why American and European Christianity Are in Such a Funk

Cascade Books
An Imprint of Wipf and Stock Publishers
199 W. 8th Ave., Suite 3
Eugene, OR 97401

www.wipfandstock.com

PAPERBACK ISBN: 978-1-5326-4962-2
HARDCOVER ISBN: 978-1-5326-4963-9
EBOOK ISBN: 978-1-5326-4964-6

Cataloguing-in-Publication data:

Names: Ellingsen, Mark, 1949–, author.

Title: Ever hear of Feuerbach? : that's why American and European Christianity are in such a funk / Mark Ellingsen.

Description: Eugene, OR : Cascade Books, 2020 | Includes bibliographical references and index.

Identifiers: ISBN 978-1-5326-4962-2 (paperback) | ISBN 978-1-5326-4963-9 (hardcover) | ISBN 978-1-5326-4964-6 (ebook)

Subjects: LCSH: Feuerbach, Ludwig, 1804–1872. | Theology.

Classification: BR115.I6 E44 2020 (paperback) | BR115.I6 E44 (ebook)

Manufactured in the U.S.A.   10/09/20

For Ali

Our newest, youngest daughter

and

for Matt and Barbara, the great folks who raised her

Contents

Acknowledgments

I have known about Ludwig Feuerbach for more than fifty years, my whole adult life, and been struggling with him all those years. Every theological move I've made, every new theological idea presented to me (including the classical options), needed to be evaluated in light of his critique of Christianity. A couple of my instructors at Gettysburg College back in the 1960s got me started, using Feuerbach to challenge my latest efforts to theologize (alas, it does not happen there anymore), but by the time I got to Yale in the early 1970s, such a dialogue with Feuerbach had become a way of life for me. Professors did not need to remind me to do it. The integrity of Christianity, the very existence of God, was at stake if I could not get around his idea that Christianity is something we humans have made up. I have been disappointed over the years that there have not been more of my colleagues who shared this worry with me. How could anyone who loves Jesus be content to see Christianity be made vulnerable to that critique? This is a book that tries to explain why Feuerbach is not a big deal to a lot of scholars and what the costs of the neglect have been. Maybe I can find some friends and allies in this struggle through this book, so that together we can perfect and find a way authoritatively to overturn the Feuerbachian critique of faith.

Along the way I've not been entirely alone. Karl Barth's reflections on Feuerbach and Barth's own style of theology have been an invaluable ally in my years of theological meandering. And I mention in the book others who have struggled with the Feuerbach critique and offered hints to me as to how to do it. Another invaluable ally for this book has been Cascade Books editor Charlie Collier, who is one of the very best with whom I've ever worked. Of course, there is one who has been with me almost as long as Barth has as an ally—the first editor of this book (and all my other twenty-two), my best friend and wife, Betsey. We've talked a lot about Feuerbach over the nearly half a century we've been together. And of course, I've had companionship from our children too. Betsey has only delivered three, but we like to say we have six children—adding the spouses of our three. The newest of these additional children is an Oregon native, Ali Spangler (now Ellingsen), whom our youngest, Peter, was wise enough to marry. Though we like to say she's ours, we can't take credit for raising her. That honor goes to her parents, Barbara and Matt Spangler, who feel like family too. How appropriate that these lifelong Oregon natives (one side of the family has Oregon Trail settler ancestors) should get this book dedicated to them, published as it is in Oregon by Wipf and Stock. I just hope my efforts in this book to cut some new theological ground for the church in our present postmodern frontier are worthy of the pioneering spirit of Ali's family roots. And so that's another reason why this book is for her.

1

Who's This German Guy, and What's He Got to Do with the Church's Funk?

Karl Barth Will Tell You

Ever hear of Ludwig Feuerbach? Know what he says about Christianity? And if you have heard of him, are his ideas on your mind a lot? Is he a conversation partner for what you do and say theologically?

My guess is that your answer to (at least most of) these questions is in the negative. And the very fact that we are not worrying a lot about this nineteenth-century German philosopher (an important influence on Karl Marx) explains why the church in Europe and America is in such a funk!

Let's begin with what all observers of religion and most theologically interested Christians know about American Christianity. American churches (especially those of the mainline) are losing ground, in terms of membership, financial resources, and social impact. The media made much of 2016 polls regarding the growth of the Nones (Americans with no religious affiliation). According to a 2017 *Washington Post*/ABC News poll, more than one in five Americans (21 percent) fall into this category.[1] In 2018, the

---

1. Reported in De Jong, "Protestants Decline, More Have No Religion."

Gallup Poll reported the number of religiously unaffiliated to be 20 percent (26 percent according to the most recent Pew Research Center survey). This is a striking increase from the late 1940s and 1950s, when, according to Gallup poll calculations, only 2 to 3 percent fell into this category. By the 1970s the number reached 10 percent. But the big growth spurt began in 1986, with a dramatic increase in the religiously unaffiliated since 2003.[2] According to a poll taken in 2019 by the Pew Research Center, four in ten young adults are religiously unaffiliated. The Pew Research Center also reported in 2018 that nearly half of Canadian young adults have no religious affiliation, and another poll found 53 percent of the British public fall into this category.[3]

Correspondingly, Gallup reports that church membership has dropped from a high of 73 percent in 1937 to 50 percent in 2018 (down from 56 percent in 2016). This has implications for reported church attendance. Reported attendance in religious services was only 23 percent in 2019 according to Statista, down from a high of 49 percent in the 1950s.[4] (Polls suggest the unreliability of these statistics. They have been and likely still are inflated, as people seem to overestimate their religiosity when polled.) Tied with these numbers is the growing sense among Americans that religion is losing influence in American society. A 2019 Pew Research Center poll reported that 78 percent of us believe this to be the case.[5]

The situation in Western Europe is worse, Gallup/International reported in 2015. In the United Kingdom only 30 percent describe themselves as religious. Germany is not much better, with 34 percent of the population perceiving themselves this way. It gets

2. "Religion," *Gallup News*; Religion News Service and *The Christian Century*, "Number of Nones Equals Evangelicals, Catholics"; Pew Research Center, "19 Striking Findings from 2019."

3. Pew Research Center, "In U.S., Decline of Christianity Continues"; Pew Research Center, "Young Adults around the World Are Less Religious"; Sherwood, "More Than Half UK Population Has No Religion, Survey Finds."

4. Statista, "Church Attendance of Americans 2019."

5. Pew Research Center, "Americans Have Positive Views About Religion's Role in Society."

worse in the Netherlands (26 percent) and bottoms out in Norway (21 percent) and Sweden (19 percent).[6] Since Christianity is the dominant (even state-sponsored) religion in these nations, the conclusion is obvious. The church is not just in a funk in Western Europe. It's on life support.

This poll data seems to confirm what Ludwig Feuerbach (1804–72) said about religion nearly two hundred years ago. Essentially what he claimed (we'll analyze how he arrived at this conclusion in more detail later) is that religion is nothing more than the objectification of who we are. We have taken the best aspects of our human nature, objectified and personified them, and then transformed the result into an object that we worship![7] If this sounds like Karl Marx and his idea that religion is a human creation, the opiate of the people, it should be no surprise. Marx expressly attributes his religious views to Feuerbach.[8]

The emerging secularism seems right in line with what Feuerbach told us. It's just the case that it took close to two centuries for Americans and Western Europeans to catch on.

There is some additional poll data, though, which the media with its secular bias has glossed over. And these poll results are precisely what makes the old German guy I've been mentioning relevant for understanding not just where we're at but also how to get out of the mess.

It seems that for all of religion's problems, a lot of Americans still think it is important in their daily lives. Gallup reported in 2019 that 75 percent of Americans feel that way.[9] A Pew Research poll taken in 2018 found that 88 percent of evangelicals felt this way about religion's importance. Likewise 88 percent of Black Christians. By contrast only 58 percent of American Catholics and 47 percent of mainline Protestants found religion essential in their

---

6. Statistics reported in O. Smith, "Mapped: The World's Most (and Least) Religious Countries."

7. Feuerbach, *The Essence of Christianity*, 12ff.

8. Marx, "Contribution to the Critique of Hegel's Philosophy of Right," 43; Marx, "Theses on Feuerbach," 83.

9. "Religion," *Gallup News*, 2019.

everyday lives.[10] These numbers parallel the fact that it is only the mainline churches that are hemorrhaging members. Pew reports that in the past decade or so "the most significant growth is [in] the nondenominational family" and that "Evangelical Protestantism and the historically Black Protestant tradition have been more stable."[11] This data suggests that theologically conservative bodies, or at least those who continue to affirm the historic positions of the faith with authority, are more successful in nurturing an active faith. The very fact that 32 percent of the Nones claim that their lack of affiliation with a religious body is associated with being reared in a childhood family that was never that religious is a further testimony to the relevance of the historic Christian faith in acting as a buffer against present sociocultural trends.[12] It is precisely at this point that the reference to famed twentieth-century Swiss theologian Karl Barth becomes relevant. He can tell us how and why we need to get around Ludwig Feuerbach's critique of religion if we want to get out of our funk.

What we will see, though, is that the dominant strands of mainline theology fall prey to Feuerbach's reduction of religion to human experience, to perceive Christianity as nothing more than a description of human states. And because Feuerbach's human-centered, secular way of viewing reality has become incarnate in Western pop culture, because we think everything we encounter is done by and for humans, that we manage everything in life, the average American and Western European hears and sees what the churches are doing in light of an uncritical Feuerbachian paradigm. Polls indicate that most Americans still believe in God, but it's their own version of God. Consequently, for many Americans it's like the best-selling author Reza Aslan says, "You are God."[13]

10. Pew Research Center, "How Does Pew Research Center Measure the Religious Composition of the U.S?"

11. Cited in "New Harvard Research Says U.S. Christianity Is Not Shrinking, But Growing Stronger."

12. Data drawn from Public Religion Research Institute and Religion News Service August 2016 survey. See Cooper et al., *Exodus: Why Americans Are Leaving Religion—and Why They're Unlikely to Come Back.*

13. On the individualism of American religion, see Twenge, *iGen,* esp.

This entails that many of the Nones (perhaps as many as 63 percent of them), but fewer and fewer of those of the Millennial generation, are spiritual but not religious.[14]

From this point of view, religion is nothing more than a rather old-fashioned, not-very-interesting set of human values, just an opinion Thomas Jefferson taught Americans to believe, a (human) crutch, a way of people fooling themselves into thinking that old-time values and lifestyles have meaning and can be rewarded.[15] In fact, polls suggest that these privatizing, subjectivist dynamics have led many to reject religious institutions because they impose too many rules on us and try to limit our choices.[16] Indeed, analysts have observed that the Nones find beliefs nonessential to spirituality.[17] With the mantra today among the Generation Xers being about maintaining independence and being "open-minded," not caring what others think, little wonder the church would be perceived as a rule-bound institution.[18]

We need an awareness of Feuerbach (especially Karl Barth's assessment of him) to help church leaders realize that the "cutting-edge" theologies and ministry paradigms they are propagating are being heard among the average citizen as Feuerbach heard them—just human proposals. This is why our churches' ignorance of Feuerbach, our silence about his critique, is so problematic. It shows that we've been doing our theology and ministry without

---

126–27, 138ff.; cf. Aslan, *God: A Human History*, 171; Mercadante, *Belief without Borders*, 134–36.

14. See the research of Mercadante, *Belief without Borders*, 32–34, cf. 93; Pew Research Center, "Why America's 'Nones' Don't Identify with a Religion"; Twenge, *iGen*, 13–132; White, *The Rise of the Nones*, 26–28.

15. Jefferson, "Bill for Establishing Religious Freedom [in Virginia]," 346; Twenge, *iGen*, 139, provides insights about how those born since the internet era began tend to reject religion on grounds of its belonging to the past, unable to address the present.

16. For data supporting this analysis, see Twenge, *iGen*, 13ff.; Twenge, *Generation Me*, 34–35.

17. See Mercadante, *Belief without Borders*, 8–9.

18. For this characterization of the Millennials, see Twenge, *Generation Me*, 24.

regard to the question of whether what the church says and does is just another human option—something people have made up in order to cope with reality. And as long as the church does not make clear in our context that her teachings are God's pronouncements, what is said and taught will be heard as just another human option that church leaders and society use to try to undermine our freedom to do what we want to do.

If the mainline churches really want to have a chance to make an impact in our present context, then, they need to begin to be perceived as offering a worldview that breaks with the usual human-centered value alternatives that saturate the public. It will require the development and use of theological models that will be heard in our individualistic ethos as making clear that Christian claims derive from an authoritative, transcendent source, not just another human opinion. Then Christians will be offering a real alternative to what everybody else can have without a faith perspective. The fact that evangelicals provide such an alternative accounts for why they and the theologically conservative African-American churches have not yet experienced the funk of their mainline partners. What would a mainline church theological and ministry option look like that would embody these virtues, breaking with the prevailing models, while still retaining intellectual credibility that an evangelical insistence on biblical infallibility does not?

This is where Karl Barth's dialogue with Feuerbach becomes relevant. We may not be able to embrace everything Barth proposed; we will need to elaborate more than he did on the idea of theology as science. Yet at least in his insistence on focusing first on the Word of God—a Word that stands over-against us—he can get us started, point us in some good directions. Barth's proposals and the importance of Feuerbach for understanding our present situation will make more sense after further elaboration on the dynamics involved in the making of our present human-centered secular ethos.

HOW DID WE GET WHERE WE ARE?

Providing a full explanation of the social causes of how the church and Western society have arrived at their present state is beyond the scope of this book. I am merely trying to explain how the church and the prevailing strands of theology and biblical studies exacerbate these trends, and how if we continue doing what we have been doing theologically and in the churches we are likely to make things worse. Besides, I don't need to spend a lot of time doing a sociological and philosophical analysis of the growing secularism in America and in Western Europe, because that job has already been done. Indeed, much of what well-known sociologist Peter Berger wrote about secularization a half-century ago is still very pertinent.

Essentially, Berger undercut the naïve belief that secularization is the polar opposite of religion, that secularization puts us on an inevitable path to the conquest of the sacred and its associated religious institutions by the profane. Rather, Berger defines secularization as a process by which sectors of society and culture are progressively removed from domination by religious institutions and symbols. Drawing on a similar but more recent analysis by Canadian philosopher Charles Taylor, we might say that secularism makes it plausible not to view all aspects of life as dependent on God. Because we are social creatures, this entails that the process has a subjective side, secularizing our consciousness.[19]

Berger's analysis of this process remains timely in our context. He suggests that the modern economy has been and continues to be the main bearer of secularizing tendencies. At the factory (but also, I would add, on the Net or in service jobs) "religion stops at the . . . gate."[20] On the job or when dealing with the products of the job or the factory (in the shopping mall or on the Net) we occupy space that is free of religion. This is in contrast to an agrarian economy, in which success (a good harvest) is seen as predicated

19. Berger, *The Sacred Canopy*, esp. 107–8. Also see C. Taylor, *A Secular Age*; J. Smith, *How (Not) to Be Secular*.

20. Berger, *The Sacred Canopy*, 129, 109.

on God's blessings and interventions. These dynamics help explain why at least until recently those on the margins of the economic system have been more religious than those who are "making it."[21] This is still the case among those who "feel" ethnically marginalized, as African-Americans and Hispanics poll as more religious than American-born whites.[22]

Berger and a more recent analysis of secularization by Charles Taylor note other features of this secularization process that are relevant for us to consider. They agree that Protestantism seems more vulnerable than Catholicism to these dynamics. The sacred is everywhere in Catholic (and, I would add, Eastern Orthodox) piety. God is everywhere in this piety, in the ordinary things of the world like bread and wine, as well as water. The miraculous Presence of Christ is evident in every worship service. Outside the sanctuary there is a global network of intercession uniting the faithful to believers all over the world, even to saints both living and those passed to the other side. Miracles, mystery, and magic are not foreign to the world of Catholics and Eastern Christians. (I would add that miracles are still real in the worlds of conservative evangelicalism and the Black church, which may help explain their persistent resistance to secular trends.) By contrast, it is argued by Berger, in many segments of (white) Protestantism (especially its Reformed branches) the sacramental and intercessory apparatus is minimized. A transcendent God is removed from the realities of everyday life. Contact with God has been narrowed, just to God's Word, accessible in religious activities. To be sure, in these traditions God is still said to be in control of earthly realities, but these realities no longer reflect the holy. And since they are not holy, as belief in a sovereign God declines in favor of human free will, it begins to seem that these ordinary realities are closed to the sacred.

21. Berger, *The Sacred Canopy*, 108.

22. See statistics of a 2009 Gallup poll reported on by Albert. L. Winseman, "U.S. Church Looking for a Few White Men." The findings of a 2015 Pew Research Center survey of "America's Changing Religious Landscape" verifies the continuing relevance of this data, as although the percentage of Christians in America declines, there has been no decline of professed Christianity among African-Americans. See footnote 11 above.

Put all these together, and it seems less and less of a disconnect, even for the faithful, to think of the job and its associated realities as secular matters.[23]

As we live more and more in this climate, religious legitimations of the world increasingly lose credibility, a dynamic that is reflected even among the faithful. And when that happens, pluralism increases, for the person in the street in a secular ethos is now confronted with a plethora of options.[24] The pluralism that confronts and seems to trouble many of us today, the celebration of pluralism that characterizes the academy and is celebrated by the media, is a direct function of the secularizing dynamics that have so successfully permeated American society since the 1960s.

Of course, our internet culture continues to provide a plethora of options that further exacerbates the pluralism, making it seem like truth is what most of our friends and influential sites say is true.[25] Ethical judgments and so religious claims are now predicated on what is good for individuals. The most recent 2017 Barna poll on the subject found that two in three Americans believe that moral truth is relative.[26] It is evident again at this point that the core suppositions of much American life exhibit many of the views of Ludwig Feuerbach.[27]

More pluralism does not make us happy, it seems. Berger points out how we are losing a sense of certainty in daily life. Maybe that is why we crave the certainty that demagogues seem to provide, why we are often so intolerant of others who challenge us,

23. Berger, *The Sacred Canopy*, 111–13. For more recent reports, see Pew Research Center, "Most U.S. Teens See Anxiety and Depression as a Major Problem Among Their Peers."

24. Berger, *The Sacred Canopy*, 124; Ammerman, *Sacred Stories, Spiritual Tales*, 301.

25. White, *The Rise of the Nones*, esp. 58ff.

26. Mercadante, *Belief without Borders*, 137ff.; cf. White, *The Rise of the Nones*, 61; Sri, *Who Am I to Judge?*, esp. 4–5.

27. Late in his career, Feuerbach referred to morality as doing what meets or drives us to seek happiness. See his "Uber Spiritualismus und Materialismus," 70–74.

and why polls indicate younger generations that have grown up in this pluralism poll as less happy.[28]

Berger makes other profound points most relevant to understanding our situation and its impact on the mainline churches in America. He observes that the modern economy is what drives secularization.[29] This is a striking observation that makes intuitive sense. The market is always prodding us to examine new possibilities and options. The premise is that these products can provide happiness, meaning, and fulfillment, precisely what faith alone used to promise. Besides, religion seems to stop at the factory gate. It is the means of production, not God, that make the products. It is we, not God, who produce the technology, the information transmitted, and most of the social connections we make have nothing to do with religion. In addition, the customization of products, of marketing, and of social media intensifies the pluralism that had earlier characterized modern life, further marginalizing religious legitimations of life.

Father Alexander Schmemann nicely defines secularism, and his remarks make even more sense in light of Berger's analysis:

> A secularist views the world as containing within itself its meaning and the principles of knowledge and action.[30]

No need for religion when the world explains itself. And it certainly does when the internet provides you with all the data you can use (and more than you need or want).

Because the world makes sense just fine without religion, even the religious values and beliefs that remain among the faithful are now matters of personal choice. Religion is merely a matter of choice or preference, not providing values that norm American and Western society's sense of right and wrong or what is socially acceptable.[31]

---

28. Berger, "Introduction," 6; Twenge, *iGen*, esp. 21ff.
29. Berger, *The Sacred Canopy*, 109, 129.
30. Schmemann, "Worship in a Secular Age," 106.
31. Berger, *The Sacred Canopy*, 133.

In this new status, Berger notes, the ethos of religious institutions like the church and its theology change significantly. This privatization of religion seems to entail that religion makes most sense when it is regarded as rooted in the individual consciousness, not in facticities of the ancient world.[32] We will observe in upcoming chapters how accurate a characterization this is of the prevailing theologies of our new century. Students of theology are already intuitively aware of the prevalence of this approach in the theological academy. The "cutting-edge theologies" of our day are little more than futile attempts to make sense of Christianity in the trivial little box in which secularism has created for it.

We will also observe in the next chapter the insight of Berger in claiming that when functioning in the context of secular pluralism religious institutions feel the need to produce results in a competitive situation. As a result, there are perceived needs in these institutions to demonstrate their efficiency and the success of their mission, often with reference to membership and stewardship statistics. The push toward efficiency entails that there are incentives for these church organizations to professionalize, to conform to prevailing business models of bureaucracy (today we would call it team management or Gut Values Connection). As we'll note in the next chapter, more and more the mainline churches in America are looking alike in their national offices.[33]

These dynamics lead Berger to conclude that the need for churches to market their product among a plethora of options entails that they must "secularize" Christianity in order that it might be attractive to the secularized consciousness of the market. As a result, Christian truth becomes consumer-controlled. This explains why there is more expressed concern with laity and lay leadership in the mainline churches than ever before.[34]

As a result of this sensitivity to the opinions of laity and to the secularized values of greater society, religious leaders become

32. Berger, *The Sacred Canopy*, 151–52.

33. Berger, *The Sacred Canopy*, 139–40; see Sosnik et al., *Applebee's America*, esp. 7.

34. Berger, *The Sacred Canopy*, 147–48.

more and more sensitized to the need to present the truths of religion and to function professionally in such a way that they speak to people, at least in ways that take the wishes and expectations of the public into account. The famed sociologist puts it this way:

> This means, furthermore, that a dynamic element is introduced into the situation, a principle of changeability if not change that is intrinsically inimical to religious traditionalism. In other words, in this situation it becomes increasingly difficult to maintain the traditions as unchanging verity. Instead, the dynamics of consumer preference is introduced into the religious sphere. Religious contents become subjects of "fashion."[35]

In Berger's view, another consequence of the churches' reactions to secularizing trends is that in marketing the gospel it becomes important to focus on its therapeutic value.[36] This clearly harmonizes with why the rooting of religious claims in the human consciousness has become, as we have already observed, the dominant way of doing theology in America and Western Europe. It also explains the dominance of the discipline of pastoral care in theological education today. Little wonder that the theology of our day is less focused on the historic doctrines of the faith, that doctrines are reinterpreted to fit or to be in dialogue with the subjective consciousness. Christian teachings are rooted in the psyche or the individual's experience. Correspondingly, theological scholarship does not help you make an impression among colleagues. It is increasingly deemed just academic. Instead, as Berger observes, "The social-psychological type emerging in the leadership of bureaucratized religious institutions is, naturally, similar to the bureaucratic personality in other institutional contexts—activist, pragmatically oriented, not given to administratively irrelevant reflection, skilled in interpersonal relations . . ."[37]

Bottom line: secularism has personalized, subjectivized faith, and the result is that in buying into this agenda in order to remain

---

35. Berger, *The Sacred Canopy*, 145–46.
36. Berger, *The Sacred Canopy*, 147.
37. Berger, *The Sacred Canopy*, 141.

relevant, the mainline churches seem to have nothing unique to offer a secular world yearning for an alternative.[38] The rest of this book will convince you of this reality and help us see what we need to do in order to get the churches out of this funk. I propose that we need to do our theology in dialogue with Ludwig Feuerbach in order to make the case that his critique does not pertain to the preaching and teaching we are doing. That way we can be sure that what we do and say regarding Christian faith is not reducing God and items of faith to human experience, so that the church and its teachings will not be perceived as just another (not too interesting) option for living.

With this analysis in hand, we are ready to examine precisely how both the analysis of religion offered by Ludwig Feuerbach and Karl Barth's reaction to it are relevant. The theology that results from secularization is precisely what they are reacting to.

THE TARGETS OF FEUERBACH AND BARTH: WE NEED CONVERSATION WITH THEM TODAY

It is hardly surprising that theology in Feuerbach's lifetime would have the characteristics of a reaction to secularism. For secularism was well underway in his context.

Academic theology in nineteenth-century Germany had largely bought the agenda of the Enlightenment. Functioning as a historian, Karl Barth nicely characterized this agenda. It involved being optimistic about humanity's ability to master life by means of our understanding. Educated people in this era would be the champion against prejudices and passions, against vice, hypocrisy, ignorance, superstition, and intolerance.[39] There was also a growing confidence in what the new technologies and media (like the daily newspaper) could contribute.

Optimism about what human beings could achieve was matched politically by the success of revolutions (in France and

---

38. Berger, *The Sacred Canopy*, 162, 166.

39. Barth, *Protestant Thought: From Rousseau to Ritschl*, esp. 11.

America) which stressed individual rights. And so we can say that the context in which theology was being done in the nineteenth century, the era in which Ludwig Feuerbach wrote, was one of an optimism about human nature and of what we can accomplish as individuals—along with suspicions of existing institutions (including suspicions about the church). The overlap between the times in which Feuerbach lived and our own are obvious.

We are indeed in a secularist ethos in which people view the world as containing within itself its meaning and the principles of knowledge and action. For most Americans and Western Europeans, the Enlightenment and science answer all humanity's questions. Polls of the Nones of our day reveal that a nineteenth-century optimism about life and human nature is the worldview of today's youth and of the Nones. All of them seem to share the belief that we (usually as individuals) can discern these meanings and principles.[40] And the dominant theology outside of evangelical circles, presented as just another "value" or opinion, does nothing to give people an alternative, provides none of the certainty science (or the media) provides. The theology that Feuerbach addressed was a lot like the prevailing theological streams of our day.

The next chapter is devoted to what is actually happening today in mainline Christian offices and the pews, not just in the seminaries. To be sure there are differences from Feuerbach's era. Secularism has had another century to impact society, the perceived pluralism is greater, though in theology, as we've noted, there are in fact few real options. Theology, Christian faith, is rooted for most everyone in the individual's experience. We shouldn't be surprised by that since a culture saturated by therapeutic models of well-being along with relativistic ways of thinking, self-expression is deemed a high value.[41] Of course theology (or biblical literacy) does not matter in most denominations anyway. I will also further describe how the trends just noted are reflecting in the

---

40. See the data provided in Mercandante, *Belief without Borders*, esp. 129ff., 231; White, *The Rise of the Nones*, 61; Twenge, *Generation Me*, esp. 50.

41. For this analysis, see Lindbeck, *The Nature of Doctrine*, 22–23.

denominational churches or among church leaders like they did in Feuerbach's era.

The next chapter also makes clear that the churches' efforts at marketing Christianity, to make faith relevant, have led them to focus more on its therapeutic or practical value than anything else. As we shall observe, this dynamic, coupled with the general decline of literacy, has effectively marginalized theology in church life, even in the schools of the mainline churches. But when you interpret faith in the categories of psychology, you still effectively perpetuate the trends of what modern theology has been doing since the nineteenth century. You continue to root Christian faith in the individual's experience, and if you use the kind of psychology that dominates in most mainline churches today, you endorse the optimism about what humans are capable of accomplishing that Ludwig Feuerbach was finding in the theology of his day.

Feuerbach's critique of religion is not only pertinent to the theology of our era. As we've noted, his contention that the truths of religion are rooted in our own experience, are assertions that we make up to help us cope, is to some extent a valid way of categorizing how the Nones and American society as a whole (as a result of media images) view religion.

After making all these points in the next chapter a bit clearer about why Feuerbach's critique of religion still matters today, we'll be ready in chapters 4 and 5 to consider that critique in detail and how it applies directly to America today, and then finally to sketch hitherto unexamined alternatives that would allow us boldly and attractively to talk about faith in ways that make clear God-talk is about an objective, transcendent reality. Maybe with that kind of theology, by the grace of God we'll see American and European Christianity get out of its funk!

2

What's Happening Today in Church Life?

Losing Ground since the 1960s

We have already referred to the problems American Christianity faces, its steady numerical decline since the 1960s. The hard facts are even more striking. It is little wonder that the religiously unaffiliated would be growing in view of statistics on membership losses in the mainline denominations. For example, The Episcopal Church has dropped from 3.4 million members in 1960 to 1.8 million in 2020. A more than 50 percent membership loss plagued the United Church of Christ in the same period (going from 2 million members to 800,000), and an even more marked decrease is evidenced in comparing the present membership of the Presbyterian Church (USA) (1.35 million in 2018) to the total membership of its predecessor bodies in 1960 (4.1 million). United Methodists have not done quite as poorly but still have lost ground (from 10.7 million to 6.6 million), and even less of a membership loss was endured by American (formerly Northern) Baptists (from 1.5 million to 1.15 million). The largest body of Lutherans, the Evangelical Lutheran Church in America, went from 5.3 million members in its predecessor bodies in 1960 to 3.4 million in 2020. Numerous other examples pertaining to

all the mainline denominations associated with the large membership losses could be cited.

It is true that the Catholic Church actually gained members,
from 42 million in 1960 to 72 million today. But if we exclude Hispanic immigration it looks more like a membership loss among
native-born Americans. Likewise, the largest, theologically conservative body in the US, the Southern Baptist Convention, has
grown—from 9 million to just over 15 million. But for reasons we
shall point out later in the book, in recent years the membership
growth has leveled off.

The historic Black denominations have not been as dramatically impacted. This is evident insofar as the vast majority (71 percent) of the Nones are white and only 9 percent are Black.[1] We will
talk later about some of the reasons why the Black church may
not be in quite the funk that the mainline churches are. In part, it
is a function of the fact that historic African-American denominations may not reflect all the characteristics of the mainline denominations described in this chapter. I'm going to suggest, then,
that these denominations may gain some insights from character-
istically African-American hermeneutical styles about theological
moves that can stem membership attrition and the growth of the
Nones.

Not surprisingly, church attendance is down in American
Christianity as a whole. The Gallup organization found a 9 percent
decline between 2008 and 2017 while the US population increased
16 million in this period. The Hartford Institute of Religion Research identifies that less than 20 percent of Americans are in
church weekly as of 2016, and a 2019 survey of Statista estimated it
was 23 percent. Things are not much better in Canada.[2] According
to Pew surveys, Catholic attendance has decreased from 75 percent in 1955 to 39 percent in 2017. And of course in Europe the attendance crisis is even more notable. Pew Research surveys (and it

---

1. For these statistics, see White, *Rise of the Nones*, 21–22.

2. Hartford Institute of Religion Research, "Facts About American Religion." Statista, "Church Attendance of Americans 2019"; Pew Research Center,
"5 Facts about Religion in Canada."

is verified that many self-reported churchgoers in polls exaggerate their actual involvement in worship) indicate that only 10 percent of German citizens, 12 percent of the French, and 8 percent in the UK worship weekly. Italian polls indicate the figure is 37 percent.[3] It is not a healthy portrait of the Western church we are painting. Why? What are the causes of the Western church's problems? As already suggested, these denominations have bought into models for theology and ministry which draw on the very suppositions which led Ludwig Feuerbach (whom we've already met in the first chapter) to critique Christianity and all religion as nothing more than human experience. Let's see.

DENOMINATIONAL HEADQUARTERS ETHOS

Take a trip to Nashville (United Methodist Church), Louisville (Presbyterian Church [USA]), Cleveland (UCC), New York (The Episcopal Church), Chicago (Evangelical Lutheran Church in America), and Washington (headquarters of the Catholic Bishops Conference), and things will look pretty stable and sound in these impressive denominational offices. Visit the fine facilities, staffed by good-sized professional staffs, organized in corporate-style division of labor even employing the kind of networking style used in many successful corporations, with worldwide contacts, and regional offices all over the nation, and one comes away with the impression that these are thriving organizations. Many who staff these offices have the personal traits and professional demeanor that give the impression that they could move and mix well with corporate peers. Like such peers they are often travelling and will tell you about their travels in ways that impress. In some denominations, a man's career might be helped if he has a beard. (It is true that a difference from the corporate office is evident insofar as in some of these denominations there is a devotional period every day.)

3. Pew Research Center, "How Religious Commitment Varies by Country among People of All Ages."

Even the governing boards of these denominations "look" a lot like their staffs. Ethnically there may be diversity, but everybody is pretty much the same regarding educational background, jobs, and even politics. These boards are largely comprised of people drawn from professions and managers, not from the working class. Thus at press time all twenty-two of the UCC's Board of Directors were from such backgrounds (lawyers, a judge, CEOs, a social worker, an engineer, educators, banking executives, etc.). Most lay members serving on the Executive Council of The Episcopal Church (at least sixteen of twenty) are also drawn from professions. This orientation was evident as long ago as in the 1980s in the formation of my own Evangelical Lutheran Church in America. (It is by no means a new phenomenon in these denominations.) Of the thirty-eight lay members appointed to the committee to facilitate the formation process, twenty-five held jobs associated with the class of managers and professionals. In 1989 there was much controversy about the composition of a task force on human sexuality for the new denomination, controversy about whether it was efficient to add a conservative. Only subsequently was one added, one who was "reasonable." The vocational composition of the denomination's church council continues these trends, at least as recently as 2019.

Penetrate the realities of these denominational offices, talk to staff, however, and it becomes clear that all is not well. These impressive-looking offices have been impacted by the empty pews in the congregations in the urban and rural areas that the denominational offices supervise. Staffs have been reduced, departments have been eliminated, due to the budget reductions imposed by the loss of income flow from the congregations. (Congregations are not donating as big a portion of their budgets to denominational entities due to the increased cost locally of running a church and paying its pastors.) Researchers John and Sylvia Ronsvalle have documented the decline in generosity toward the church by members. In 1968 American Christians averaged 3.11 percent of their income in gifts (less than 1/3 of a tithe); in 1985 giving had fallen to 2.6 percent, and in 2011 to 2.32 percent. A different 2018 report found the average to be 2.5 percent of American Christians' incomes (about $17 per week).[4]

Just as Americans in general have become suspicious of "big" institutions (just 33 percent of us express such trust in them, according to a 2018 Gallup poll), even the church has taken a beating in the last decade—from 52 percent really trusting church organizations in 2006 to 36 percent in 2019.[5] There has always been in some of these denominations distrust of the hierarchy, but the deeper ditches that social class differences dig today cannot be discounted.

Eminent sociologists like Charles Murray have noted that class differences in American life have manifested themselves so dramatically that the professional and working classes not only now live separately, but they have different life experiences, follow different sports, enjoy different pastimes, and consumer preferences, not to mention political preferences and work habits.[6] This segregation seems largely maintained at the denominational headquarters' level, given the fact that the professional staff largely only engages with people of their own class. Little wonder, then, that many of the working-class members of these denominations would feel further estranged from their denominations. The decline of denominational consciousness also seems related to these outcomes, and it is further driven by the new American desire for self-expression and choice.[7]

The ordinary observer might expect that leaders of these denominations would be pushing denominational consciousness and theological convictions in their churches. But in fact they tend to do just the opposite (except perhaps for Catholic bishops, but even they would not have become bishops had they been too

4. Ronsvalle and Ronsvalle, *The State of Church Giving through 2011*; Nonprofits Source, "Church and Religious Charitable Giving Statistics."

5. Newport, "Americans' Confidence in Institutions Edges Up."

6. Murray, *Coming Apart: The State of White America*, esp. 100–115.

7. That these dynamics were emerging as early as the 1980s to early twenty-first century is evidenced in the data and analysis provided by Wolfe, *Moral Freedom*, esp. 185; cf. Wuthnow, *The Restructuring of American Religion*, 88–89.

ecumenically insensitive). One of the reasons for this relates to the openness to change that is dictated by the sociological dynamics of secularization that we noted in the last chapter. When addressing pluralism church leaders are pressured to surrender traditional commitments in favor of perceived consumer preferences.

The diminishing of denominational consciousness also has to do with what it takes to "get somewhere" vocationally in American society today. In our context, where flexibility and personal skills are your way to success, this entails you need to be flexible, be willing to do most anything it takes not to antagonize others.[8] You have to be a "nice" person to get a denominational job or office in mainline Christianity, be charming, and be perceived as "pastoral" with a reputation of being a good administrator. You also should have a network of powerful allies, be gregarious with an ability to get conversations focused on you, where you've been, who you know, and what you've done. Your personal life, spiritual depth, and theological skills really don't matter as long as you're not perceived as deficient in these areas. The importance of public-speaking skills depends on the denomination, but you can't be weak in this area. For reasons we'll see later in the chapter, and depending on the denomination, you should be at least a quiet proponent of most of the politically correct positions of the university and the latest liberal trends acceptable in professional circles.

Of course, you have to articulate how you love the denominational tradition. In a few instances (especially Catholic, Lutheran, and African Methodist Episcopal churches) it is better if you were born into the tradition. But the demands of flexibility entail that you do not want to employ any theological commitments you might endorse to redirect or criticize other leaders or members of the denomination. We need to embrace diversity, be flexible, give everyone their private space (the very values that our globalized new version of capitalism demands or nurtures).[9] The only time you might use theology in a critical way would be to interpret it in

8. For this analysis of the ethos of our era and the kind of leadership style that works best as a result, see Sennett, *The Corrosion of Character*, esp. 46ff.

9. Sennett, *The Corrosion of Character*, esp. 46ff.

such a way as to invoke it in order to critique rigidity and a failure to embrace "openness" and personal freedom.

These dynamics help explain why the leadership of the mainline Protestant denominations embraces ecumenical ventures so readily, without encouraging careful study of the theology behind these agreements. In some denominations the leadership, then, seems to send the message to the constituency that denominational consciousness (and so the theology of the denomination) is not that important.

No, theology does not count much with the leadership and so does not typically have a role in shaping denominational life. My own Evangelical Lutheran Church is a good example.[10] For example, the very motto of the denomination, "God's work, Our hands," has been challenged by a number of the denomination's theologians. (Luther actually claimed that creatures are "the hands of God," emphasizing that we bring nothing to God's work, not even our hands.[11]) But no response is ever made from denominational headquarters. Indeed, I have firsthand reports that staff in these offices refer to theologians of the denomination as the "theological cops."

The denomination is not even apparently open to considering scholarship. I was told by a previous editorial staff member of the denomination's old magazine *The Lutheran* that it would not consider articles on the most recent scientific assessments of whether homosexuality is genetically determined (some prominent scholars say it is not). No doubt it was feared that such inquiry would reopen the debate over gay ordinations and gay marriage that has divided the denomination.[12] So much for Socrates and the quest for truth.

10. In making this assessment I follow the insights of an eminent theologian of the denomination, Carl Braaten, in *Because of Christ: Memoirs of a Lutheran Theologian*, 127.

11. Luther, *The Large Catechism*, I.1 (389).

12. No less eminent a scientist than the head of the Human Genome Project, Francis Collins, argues that sexual orientation is not biologically determined. F. Collins, *The Language of God*, 260. For more details on the denomination's reactions to my proposal, see my article, "The ELCA's Recent

Other mainline Protestant denominations seem to reflect this neglect of theology.[13] We can see this to some extent in their recent programming. The American Baptist churches have been focusing on social justice and community development. My own Lutheran denomination targeted homosexuality, HIV, justice for women, and attended to racial issues. The Catholic Church has focused on bringing back lapsed members. United Methodism also stressed health programming and overcoming poverty. Most recently it has become focused on dividing the denomination over issues of gay rights and the ordination of practicing gays. Meanwhile the UCC targeted environmental justice and immigrant ministry. The Presbyterian Church (USA) has been focusing on homosexuality, Latino ministry, health programming, and evangelism.

All of these programs are valid and many are important. But it is striking that there were no programmatic emphases by these churches related to theology. True, the Evangelical Lutheran Church in America did recognize the Reformation's five-hundredth anniversary in 2017. But the denominational office failed to associate any theological themes with the celebration, to explore theologically why the Reformation happened and of what use it is today. True, it does now refer to equipping the baptized to communicate its theology in compelling ways, but the programming to that end is not visible at press time and as we have noted the denomination's track record on that score is not very good.[14]

Another glaring example of the neglect of theology in these denominational offices is evident in a 2019–2020 telephone survey I undertook of who in these Protestant denominational headquarters was authorized to monitor theological trends or to investigate the causes of the membership decline and growth of the religiously

Decisions in Luther of Scientific Research."

13. Elizabeth Achtemeier was reported as making a similar critique of the Presbyterian Church (USA) two decades ago by Richard Neuhaus; see "Presbyterians: Where Have All the People Gone?" Thomas Oden, in *A Change of Heart*, lamented the bankruptcy of Methodist theological education. See the websites of each of these denominations for the programmatic emphases noted, some of which may be somewhat modified by press time.

14. Evangelical Lutheran Church in America, "The Five Goals."

unaffiliated population in America. It was startling to learn that no one in any of these denominations was officially authorized to undertake these tasks or advise the hierarchy about them. Many of the denominational executives with whom I spoke (all but two requested anonymity, which says a lot about the ethos of mainline church life) lamented the decline in membership, asserting that we need more effective evangelism strategies geared to the Millennial generations. But only in three mainline denominations (the Presbyterian Church [USA], the Episcopal Church, and the Evangelical Lutheran Church in America) have such programs been implemented.

In line with the best practices of reaching Millennials and Generation Z as well as modern marketing practices, these programs are not administered by denominational offices (top-down administration). Rather, they are locally driven, endeavor to identify communities already existing or that can be formed around common interests (clubs, drinking partners, young mothers, and a myriad of interest groups), discern a navigator who might coordinate the group's spiritual quests, and then see what happens. The training sessions for starting such target groups and reports from the groups (at least those with Lutheran and Presbyterian support) are concerned with practice, not with how what is done in these groups relates to theology.[15] But when you engage in ministry with the experience of the group as your starting-point, without first interpreting theologically what is going on, you can easily lapse into the style of theology prevailing in the mainline academy which I'll be critiquing.

15. Ruben Duran, Telelphone Interview, June 29, 2020; Nikki Collins, Telephone Interview, July 1, 2020; cf. Sosnik et al., *Applebee's America*, 99ff. It is true that the Christian Church (Disciples of Christ) had a program similar to the ones described, but it predated discussion of the challenges posed by the use of the Nones, and so did not directly target this audience. The Lutheran program seemed aware of a book on new ways to preach to the Nones offered in 2007 by Nathan Frambach, *Emerging Ministry*, esp. 36ff. But this work, as we'll see, endorses the prevailing theological trends to be criticized in what follows and throughout this book.

Interestingly, one executive of the Evangelical Lutheran Church, not that program's director, even praised the theological developments that this book shows have gotten us in our present mess. A national officer of The Episcopal Church echoed these sentiments, speaking of the fluidity of sacred and secular. And although the director of the Presbyterian program offered theological reflections in our conversation on God working in places we don't expect, failure to link these suppositions to an awareness of God's sovereignty could easily be taken as reducing God's ways to our ways.

Start with the humanist suppositions about Western society and the Nones regarding how good and whole human experience is, interpret Christianity in that light, and you are likely to end up teaching a version of spirituality that is nothing more than a "religious" way of talking about present worldviews of the West and its Nones. And if the religious community in which we participate adds no fresh transcendent experiences to life, why stick with such a community? Thus to date, significantly less than one-sixth of these community starts have become permanent congregations.

The de-emphasis of theology at the denominational level reflects the reticence of leadership to employ their denominational theological heritage to play a role in criticizing illicit denominational endorsements of the latest cultural trends. This is a major part of the reason, I contend, why American Christianity and Western Christianity in particular are in such a funk. Mainline denominations look too much like a mirror of the liberal trends in society, and they are not as interesting as our secular equivalents. Consequently, we lose ground, precisely because there is not much different about us compared to the world, and we seem rather boring and uninteresting at that.

Things are not much different at the regional office level. Though the states in which the regional offices are located can make a difference, generally speaking the same kind of leadership style that is reflected in national offices characterizes staff in these offices. And because leaders at the regional level often aspire to national influence, they are not typically inclined to challenge denominational trends, for they want to stay on the good side of national church leadership. Consequently, these local leaders are not likely to challenge national church programs with theological critique nor to do theology in a style different from the denominational leadership.

The local leaders do have clout over the pastors in the region, both in terms of ordination and in terms of their promotions. Not surprisingly, when we move to the parish level a lot of the dynamics observed in national offices surface in the pulpit and the pews. I have firsthand experience in the Evangelical Lutheran Church in America with observing or being the recipient of advice given to theologically passionate candidates for ministry or pastors in their first call to chill out about all that theology, and to become more "pastoral," for people are not interested in theological issues, the mentors advise.

Visit the congregations of the mainline denominations. Catholic parishes excluded, you are unlikely to hear much preaching on the denomination's theological heritage or even on the classical doctrines like the Trinity or even the Sacraments. Instead, you will probably hear some nice secular stories or references to the pastor's or the congregation's experience, which are in turn related to the preaching text in some way.

Why this neglect of theology rooted in the tradition? The leadership's atheological dispositions are rooted in the institutional, sociological dynamics I have been describing, but the theological training and ethos of the academy are the real enablers of the mess in which the mainline churches find themselves. And so we now turn to tell that part of the story.

WHAT'S BEEN HAPPENING IN THEOLOGICAL EDUCATION

American theological education entered a heyday era after the Second World War, but there were signs of it happening even after the First World War. Until that time American theology had largely depended on European scholarship. True enough, American scholars had begun to study cutting-edge insights of

Enlightenment German theology as early as 1815. But until after the Second World War you had to study at the same Ivy League institutions or other prominent seminaries of the Northeast (Princeton was a notable exception) in order to find schools where their graduates were exposed to this "radical" thinking. Lutheran, Catholic, and denominational seminaries notably resisted these trends, rejecting use of historical criticism, or theologians and historians indebted to the philosophy of G. W. F. Hegel and others like Friedrich Schleiermacher who sought to interpret the faith in dialogue with our own experience or other worldviews.[16]

Unless you matriculated at the progressive northeastern institutions, you only studied the Bible, biblical languages, and theology. The authority of Scripture, if not its inerrancy, was widely accepted. Homiletics was being taught as a separate course at Yale in the nineteenth century. But a distinct Department of Pastoral Studies or Practical Theology was not established at the school until 1900. (In Europe it was not until 1924 that Practical Theology was endorsed as a distinct discipline at the University of Edinburgh.)

In order to appreciate what drove change and why it matters we need to examine two different though related dynamics. Before World War II the vast majority of pastors in America were not seminary-trained (especially Methodists and Baptists, not to mention those not part of mainline bodies). But with the GI Bill came a new push from almost all these denominations to "professionalize" the ministry. This translated into the need to have candidates for ministry educated. Traditions that had not previously mandated an educated clergy now began insisting on it. This and the realities of how you could avoid the draft for the Vietnam War if a candidate for ministry swelled enrollments in church colleges and seminaries in the 1960s. Also, Religious Studies departments were increasingly instituted in public colleges.

These developments were transpiring at a time when the ethos of the academy was changing. As noted, the elite or more

16. For more details, see Ahlstrom, *A Religious History of the American People*, 763ff.; Nelson et al., *The Lutherans in North America*, 381–85, 432–34.

progressive American institutions had been working with German Enlightenment thinking since the nineteenth century. They were instructing their students to take seriously Immanuel Kant's turn to the subject (the belief that we can never find absolute truth but only interpret things from the viewpoint of our own experience). Students were also taught how Hegel had made history a way to truth, and instruction in biblical studies involved a critical attempt to reconstruct the historical circumstances that gave rise to the biblical text studied. This was cutting-edge scholarship.[17] But after the Second World War the German invasion of the American university took a more full-scale, radical form. And it largely vanquished, as the famed social commentator Allan Bloom contends. In his view, what happened in the first two decades of the postwar era was that social sciences derived from German scholarship essentially came to dominate and catch the fancy of students.[18] Psychologist Sigmund Freud, sociologist Max Weber (Ernst Troeltsch at least in some seminaries), and through them Friedrich Nietzsche, a teacher of nihilism and the source of the idea of the death of God, who had influenced these scholars, became the subjects of much attention for students.[19] (We might add existentialist philosophy to this list.)

These scholars and their disciplines could only be applied to theological education if Christianity and/or religion in general were studied critically, if the Bible and theological concepts were interpreted in light of history, social currents, or feelings and mental states. Of course this approach to the Bible and theology had earlier been introduced in the academy. And with the introduction of the study of religion to state universities, these disciplines could be readily applied if religion was interpreted as human phenomenon, as human experience.

17. Kant, *Critique of Pure Reason*, 257ff.; Hegel, *Preface to the Phenomenology of the Spirit*, III.3; Strauss, *Life of Jesus, Critically Examined*, 69–70, 892–96; Wellhausen, *Prolegomena zur Geschichte Israels*.

18. Bloom, *The Closing of the American Mind*, esp. 148–49.

19. Nietzsche, *Thus Spoke Zarathustra*, Prologue 2–3.

Applying the new social scientific disciplines to theology made sense in other ways. The stress on professionalization of the clergy, on an educated clergy, after the war gave impetus for the church to adopt these exciting new disciplines. Many seminary students of the late forties and fifties had been exposed to these exciting ideas in their college years, and so it was quite natural that they would embrace ways of critically reading the Bible and seeking to find ways to integrate the insights of psychology and sociology into their faith. And when this generation came to leadership positions in the mainline churches in the 1960s and 1970s it is hardly surprising that this is when most of the mainline denominations, at least at the national office level, took their focus off historic Christianity and a conservative understanding of the Bible. Baby Boomers shepherded by these mentors, and further radicalized against anything traditional, quite naturally followed their mentors in their ordination process and also when they came to denominational leadership in the eighties through this decade. With less reflection on and guidance from authoritative biblical and doctrinal teachings, these denominations came to be more directed by the feelings of their members and by theories of institutional management.

Other dynamics encouraged these developments. As we moved into the 1960s, "relevance," distrust of the establishment, "doing your own thing" (and so breaking with the past) became the great mantras of the day, aided by the economic and secularizing trends noted in the first chapter. These dynamics prodded denomination leaders to preoccupy themselves and their churches with being relevant.

Faced with so many pressing issues (civil rights, stirrings of feminism, and Vietnam), the mainline churches joined these crusades (late) and many of the intellectual currents of the day as well—at Emory University, even the death of God! All of these dynamics along with the growing impact of relativism and the mandate to embrace pluralism (related to the saturation of the American university system by Kantian suppositions) led to a de-emphasis of evangelism and mission work in American and European church life. After all, the nonbeliever's worldview may be just as good for him as Christianity is for churchgoers on such grounds, and these attitudes began reflecting in denominational offices and pastoral leadership. Immediately after World War II Neo-Orthodox theologians like Karl Barth and Reinhold Niebuhr had their influence on church-related campuses. (This was a movement aiming to recover biblical authority in a fresh, Reformation-like way and avoid Feuerbach's critique of the faith.) But these approaches never had a real impact on the denominational leaders and so not on the pews.

The mainline pew in the postwar era remained largely theologically conservative except for the highly educated congregations that had various members inclined not to take the Bible so literally. This group would come to find the new liberal ideas younger pastors were bringing from the seminaries attractive, and in many working-class congregations, pastors trained this way to do theology in your context merely bought into the cultural assumptions of the community served without much critical theological reflection on these mores.

During these decades seminaries themselves were caught up in these dynamics. The desire for relevance encouraged faculties in the practical departments to focus not just on homiletics and church administration but also on counseling (psychology) and community action (sociology). Students, as previously noted, had incentives to gravitate towards these courses (perceiving them as relevant, where the action is). (Later, education courses and specialists were added to these departments. And with the drive for professionalization in the denominations, more attention was given to administration, so that courses in management came to find their way into the seminary curriculum.) Professors in the practical fields also came to be the most popular and influential faculty on campus. In time, since the 1960s, this has led to the phenomenon that more and more seminary presidents have their expertise in these fields, rather than in the classical disciplines, and so give the practical fields more weight in the seminaries over which they preside.

Meanwhile, the classical disciplines of biblical studies, theology, ethics, and church history became more and more marginalized. The latter two, like biblical studies, had been part of theology prior to the earliest stirrings of German Enlightenment influence. In the German homeland, the stress on making these disciplines "scientific" had led to the conviction that history and biblical studies need to be set free from the biases of theology. The result of these distinctions between or separations among these disciplines led to the creation of distinct expertises. With this dynamic the establishment of Christian ethics as a field distinct from theology made perfect sense.

With these separated fields, students of the late fifties and to this day, already inclined to seek what is relevant (practical courses), came to regard the classical disciplines as "academic," not where the action is if you want to be a pastor. Theology is the big loser, because in most cases students will gravitate towards the biblical department prior to the others (though ethics has a chance to attract those coming to seminary with social concerns, yet they might find the sociology of religion course more immediately relevant). Theology's influence was then further undercut by these dynamics because with the Enlightenment influence exerting ever more impact on biblical studies, faculty in this department more and more posed themselves as "scientific" (in the sense of being engaged in historical research), not biased like theology.

Seminaries and church colleges typically design curriculum to have incoming students take their Bible courses at the outset of their matriculation. And of course new students will most of the time gravitate to these courses prior to theology or church history courses (more often than not they have never heard of theology prior to entering the program). What they learn in these courses is how to read the Bible critically, some for the first time. The historical and scientific truth of these texts is challenged. Since the Bible is where the action is for these students, and since these scholars are providing facts to them about how the Bible cannot mean what it says, students bring this liberal orientation with them to theology classes. The result is that they either dismiss what they learn in theology and church history as speculation, as merely academic, or they dismiss theological options they learn that are rooted in the tradition (these can't be correct because the critical version of biblical studies does not vindicate them—a recent version of New Testament studies argues that the Protestant Reformers misread Paul) and so gravitate to more liberal, innovative theological options.[20] This is the problem with and the learning outcome of the prevailing curriculum in mainline seminaries.

The hidden secret that everybody understands is that the vast majority of biblical scholars portraying themselves as objective scholars of the Bible are effectively doing theology, not offering the descriptive interpretation of the biblical texts that they purport to be offering. As a result, biblical scholarship in the American academy effectively perpetuates the dominant theology of the West since the Enlightenment, one that demands that every theological and biblical affirmation be related to and evaluated by contemporary experience and its worldview. However, this theology emanating from Bible departments is done without the critical reflection on what the professor proposes constructively and without attention to historical precedents with which members of the theology department operate. Students nurtured in this curriculum come to make the prevailing liberal theology of the West as their own, but in an uncritical way and perhaps without even realizing it.

Of course the average seminary or religiously interested college student, as well as the young pastor, nurtured this way is likely to perceive what is learned in these biblical courses as too liberal, and the pastors will not share it in the churches or even believe it. As a result, all these constituencies will consider or preach the Bible less, and see faith and ministry more in terms of the concrete, practical things they have learned in practical theology courses, focusing on the social-scientific insights gained, lifestyle issues, business-management techniques, or the latest interesting

20. For a similar assessment, see Jenson, *Canon and Creed*, esp. 119. Critiques of the Reformation reading of Paul have been formulated by Dunn, *The New Perspective on Paul*, 98–101, 115–16; and N. T. Wright, *What Saint Paul Really Said*, 113–33.

wisdom/trend of pop culture. This agenda sounds like what typifies a mainline church meeting and the programmatic planning in the average urban and suburban mainline congregation. Training candidates for ministry in this ethos, it is hardly surprising that this has become the agenda for most mainline denominations.

FROM THE NEO-ORTHODOX ERA TO THE DAWN OF TODAY

Seminary life was a little different, at least for some students, at the height of Neo-Orthodox theological influence just before World War II and into the mid-1980s. Although, as we have noted, this movement has not successfully permeated the parishes, it did help nurture some pastors in the mainline churches in this era who displayed a real love of their denominational heritage and of the historic Christian tradition. It is the generation that stirred many of the advances in post-Vatican II bilateral ecumenical dialogues and created a love for doing theology among some of their Baby Boomer students. Besides Princeton and Yale, these dynamics transpired in some denominational seminaries like Wesley, Columbia (in suburban Atlanta), Gettysburg Lutheran, Concordia Lutheran (prior to a fundamentalist revolt), and Luther Seminary, just to name a few.

Of course, when one speaks of the Neo-Orthodox era, we speak of not just Barth, the Niebuhr brothers, Emil Brunner, or Hans Küng. A movement in biblical studies called Biblical Theology was also associated with it. This was a style of biblical studies that like Barth employed historical-critical tools, but also believed that God revealed himself in history and that the Bible has a theological dimension. As a result, these scholars did not overturn the coherence of the Bible's testimony or the truth of historic Christian assertions.[21]

---

21. Proponents of this approach included G. Ernest Wright, *God Who Acts*; Filson, *The New Testament against Its Environment*; von Rad, *Old Testament Theology*; Cullmann, *Christ and Time*.

The Neo-Orthodox movement also included Paul Tillich and Rudolf Bultmann (and an existentialist reading of Søren Kierkegaard), whose theologies were also heirs of the earlier liberal theologians who interpreted the Word in light of human experience. They also received a lot of attention. These theologies could lead students towards endorsing a more learned vision of the prevailing, experientially-oriented pop theologies of their denominations. But probably the majority of the students even in this era were nurtured as we have been describing, more influenced by the practical courses, which along with the critical approach to the Bible sent the message that theology is academic and will not help you much in the parish. And for that reason they were internalizing and later propagating as ordained leaders a version of Christianity not wedded to a literal reading of Scripture, not inclined to draw on theological insights to understand the world. These pastors left seminary without tools for critiquing the way the church and the world are, because their view of faith is inextricably linked to sociology, psychology, business-management techniques, or the latest trend in pop culture.

There was another unintended consequence of the kind of spiritual nurturing mainline seminaries offer and the theological orientation that they (often unwittingly) produce. When you have an undergraduate and graduate degrees and take your bearings theologically from your own experience, then it further exacerbates the class divide between clergy and many working-class laity that has always characterized denominations with an educated clergy to some extent. In some respects the mainline denominations suffer from some of the same dynamics that plague the Democratic Party, and for the same reasons.[22] They are losing the masses (especially of the working class) because their orientation comes more from professional classes and their concerns. The issues that concern working-class Christians are not typically those of self-care, flexibility, liberation, gay rights, ecology, and mutliculturalism that so occupy the official rhetoric of the mainline churches and their spokespersons. Likewise the intellectual issues and concern with

22. See Frank, *Listen, Liberal.*

personal fulfillment and creative control which shape theology in the seminaries are not the issues of the working family tired from a hard day on the job, worried about job security, and the discontent with life caused by the tension seen between what's on screen and what life in the hood or in the small town is like. In that sense these churches are not churches of the people.

The American and Western European preoccupation with subjectivity, entitlement, and doing your own thing entails that when Christianity is presented as an option for our situation, one that can meet our needs like most mainline churches do, but is not presented unambiguously as objective divine truth, the public (and especially Nones) are likely to hear this version of the Word as another private opinion that someone (those Christians) is trying to impose on us. And the public does not like someone trying to put their agenda on us.[23] Besides, Christianity does not seem like a very interesting option anyway, especially when you compare it to titillating virtual realties and other forms of entertainment available.

Fundamentalist or theologically conservative churches are at least somewhat insulated from these problems of proclaiming a version of the Word estranged from the experience of the faithful precisely because they teach a version of the Word that is in principle accessible to all and binding on all, and so it is not as dependent on the peculiar ways the preacher or the denominational executives "read" the world. It is striking how irrelevant the mainline churches have made themselves while seeking relevance. And we can now see, the theology which is prevailing in these churches has been a big cause of the problems.

Wait! It even gets worse. This chapter has only taken you as far as the last twelve to fifteen years of the twentieth century. And it's only gotten worse for the mainline churches since then. We will tell that story in more detail in chapter 4, after becoming even clearer what is at stake in the mainline churches' embracing of the kind of Enlightenment style of liberal theology that they have. What's worse, as we'll next see, is that the dominant theology

23. See Twenge, *Generation Me*, 34–35.

in the seminaries we have been describing now pretty much has a monopoly in those settings and in college religion departments with the fading of the influence of Karl Barth and Neo-Orthodox theology in these settings. And so it's no surprise that things have gotten worse in the mainline churches in the last twenty years or so. But first we need to become clearer on what is at stake theologically in these developments. We can see this more clearly by taking a detailed look at the philosopher Ludwig Feuerbach's critique of the theology of his day, a theology a lot like what dominates in the mainline today, and then carefully observe Karl Barth's critique of this theology and his formula for overcoming it. What follows, then, also will be a chapter about what the mainline denominations need to start doing to overcome the theology that dominates them in order to get out of their funk.

3

A Detailed Look at Feuerbach
and Barth's Critique

Since I am trying to say that our ignorance and neglect of Ludwig Feuerbach and his critique of Christianity is an important factor in the funk experienced by mainline churches in the West, I'd better provide a fuller introduction to this nineteenth-century German scholar.

We've already been introduced a little to Feuerbach's context and talked about his influence on Karl Marx as left-wing students of the great German philosopher G. W. F. Hegel. But this young Bavarian, born in 1804 as the son of an eminent jurist, was not your typical atheist. He went to university to study theology, intending a career in the ministry! What happened?

Gradually, the budding pastor/theologian came to study with the famed Hegel. The mission of Feuerbach's intellectual mentor was to take seriously his predecessor Immanuel Kant's claim that the mind stamps its seal on all reality.[1] Kant, as we shall see, is the real philosophical mentor of the theology that dominates in the mainline churches today, which has dominated modern theology

---

1. Hegel, *Phenomenology of Spirit*, Pref.II.2–3.

since his lifetime.[2] For Kant's way of understanding how we know (epistemology) entails that all interpretation and knowledge are the work of the interpreter's contribution. We impose our own experience, make a creative contribution to everything we know.

Hegel was determined to move beyond Kant in positing an ontology whereby Reason is reality itself. Such a belief in the rational character of reality entails that when one thinks, one is in touch with reality itself, with Being-itself. It follows, then, that one best knows the other by becoming subjective, for the other is essentially related to the One to which the knower and his/her subjectivity belongs.[3]

To these points Hegel added the concept of the *Dialectic* (a process, ever moving, from Thesis to Antithesis to Synthesis). Not only is this the way we think at our best, in his view. The Dialectic is also universal Reason (Being or the Spirit). The whole of reality, then, is in process, moving towards ultimate divine-human identity.[4]

Hegel proceeded to interpret Christian faith in light of his philosophical suppositions. He regarded the content of both as the same.[5] Theology turns into philosophy, he claimed. Religion is only necessary due to the variance of the spiritual necessities of men. Through Reason we can understand the claims of Christian faith—that the divine and human in Christ provide a pictorial view of the history of the Divine Idea actualizing the implicit unity of divine and human.[6]

This vision entails that history is to be taken with utmost seriousness, because insofar as it embodies the Dialectic it reveals the substance of Reason and eternal reality. The lesson history teaches,

2. For this assessment, see Dorrien, *Kantian Reason and Hegelian Spirit*, esp. 2ff.; Bloesch, *A Theology of Word & Spirit*, 25–26; Dillenberger and Welch, *Protestant Christianity Interpreted through Its Development*, 213; Davidovich, *Religion as a Province of Meaning*.

3. Hegel, *Phenomenology of Spirit*, Pref.III.1.

4. Hegel, *Lectures on the History of Philosophy*.

5. Hegel, *Lectures on the Philosophy of Religion*, III.II.1.

6. Hegel, *Lectures on the Philosophy of Religion*, II.II.3; Hegel, *Amplification of the Teleological Proof*.

it seems, is that Life is about sacrificing itself in order to become Spirit.[7] The aim of personhood then seems to be, as illustrated in the Trinity, to annihilate itself in the essence of the Godhead.[8] For as we have noted, for Hegel God is Being-Itself.[9]

Marx and other left-wing Hegelians wanted to maintain Hegel's system without all the spiritual and speculative dimensions it promulgated. After all, his mentor was teaching that through human means (Reason) we can attain all that the Word of God offers.

In this light, Feuerbach began with an attack of the idea of personal immortality.[10] It was just an aspect of what became his overriding agenda, to change "the friends of God into friends of man, believers into thinkers, worshippers into workers, candidates for the other world into students of this world, Christians, who on their own confession are half-animal and half-angel, into men—whole men."[11] To this scenario he added a desire to change "theologians into anthropologians . . . religious and political footmen of a celestial and terrestrial monarchy and aristocracy into free, self-reliant citizens of earth."[12]

In this 1841 book on which we will focus, *The Essence of Christianity*, Feuerbach puts out a call: turn away from a lie to truth, from god to the world! He calls us to help us secure our due.[13] He begins his reflections by distinguishing us from animals, claiming in line with Hegelian thinking that we have a consciousness that is aware of ourselves as a species, of an essential nature. We are at once both I and Thou. We can put ourselves in the place of another. This is why our essential nature, not just our individuality, can be an object of thought.[14]

7. Hegel, *Lectures on the Philosophy of Religion*, III.II.2.

8. Hegel, *Lectures on the Philosophy of Religion*, III.I.3.

9. Hegel, *Lectures on the Proofs of the Existence of God*, 10.

10. Feuerbach, "Thoughts on Death and Immortality."

11. Feuerbach, *Das Wesen der Religion*, 170.

12. Feuerbach, *Das Wesen der Religion*, 14.

13. For these insights about Feuerbach's aims I am indebted to Karl Barth, "An Introductory Essay," in Feuerbach, *The Essence of Christianity*, xii–xiii.

14. Feuerbach, *The Essence of Christianity*, 1–4.

Feuerbach goes on to add that without an object of our thought, we are nothing. The greatest human beings have been those who devoted all their activity to their one passion.[15] Then he adds,

> In the object which he contemplates, therefore, man becomes acquainted with himself; consciousness of objective is the self-consciousness of man. We know by the object, by his conception of what is external to himself; in it his nature becomes evident.... And this is true not merely of spiritual, but also of sensuous objects. Even the objects which are the most remote from man, *because* they are objects to him . . . are revelations of human nature.[16]

We see strong Kantian commitments in these comments—that we can never get to objects in themselves but only perceive them from our own perspectives. To this, in line with Hegelianism, Feuerbach adds, "But the object to which a subject essentially relates, is nothing else than this subject's own, but objective nature."[17]

This philosophical background providing the framework for interpreting Christianity leads Feuerbach to his controversial conclusions. Because the individual cannot exist apart from his recognition of the species and cannot conceive of another level of existence that does not possess human qualities, the implications regarding God are inevitable: "Religion—consciousness of God—is designated as the self-consciousness of man. . . . Man first of all sees his nature as if *out of* himself, before his finds it in himself."[18]

The religious object of adoration is just the objectified nature of human beings, but we don't realize it. Feuerbach hastens to make it clear that the Christian God is not merely the objectified nature of the individual but rather has attributed to it all the potentialities of the human species:

---

15. Feuerbach, *The Essence of Christianity*, 4.
16. Feuerbach, *The Essence of Christianity*, 5.
17. Feuerbach, *The Essence of Christianity*, 4.
18. Feuerbach, *The Essence of Christianity*, 12–13.

> The divine being is nothing else than the human being, or, rather, the human nature purified, freed from the limits of the individual man, made objective—i.e., contemplated and revered as another, a distinct being. All the attributes of the divine nature are, therefore, attributes of the human nature.[19]

With this understanding of God in hand, Feuerbach believes that he has unlocked what religion is all about—humanity's goodness and happiness. In fact, he adds that in religion we seek contentment.[20] Is that not a lot like the way we regard religion in our therapeutic, self-fulfillment ethos today?

> Man—this is the mystery of religion—projects his being into objectivity, and then again makes himself an object to this projected image of himself thus converted into a subject; he thinks of himself as an object. . . . That man is good or evil is not indifferent to God. . . . Thus man has in fact no other aim than himself. The divine activity is not distinct from the human.[21]

What we attribute to God is just our own activity objectified.[22] This is the tragedy of religion. It alienates us from ourselves, setting up God as the antithesis of who we are. When in fact we are capable as a species of being who God is if we devoted ourselves to that task. Likewise the religious mind makes itself passive while deeming God active being, when in fact man is the religious subject. In revelation we go out of ourselves in order, by a circuitous route, to return to ourselves. For the faithful say that divine revelation and human reason are distinct, and yet the contents of divine revelation are of human origin.[23] Such a belief poisons the most divine feeling in human beings—the quest for truth.[24]

19. Feuerbach, *The Essence of Christianity*, 14; cf. 213.

20. Feuerbach, *The Essence of Christianity*, 45.

21. Feuerbach, *The Essence of Christianity*, 29–30.

22. Feuerbach, *The Essence of Christianity*, 30–31.

23. Feuerbach, *The Essence of Christianity*, 206–7.

24. Feuerbach, *The Essence of Christianity*, 209.

Feuerbach's project was not intended to be purely negative, to diminish theology and religion. He contends that he is concerned "to make God real and human."[25] For example, we are isolated by faith in God, for it makes God a particular, distinct being. Faith also gives man a peculiar sense of his own dignity, that he is exalted above natural men and unbelievers. But with the love that Feuerbach's interpretation of religion helps us to see, the preoccupation with the isolated ego in religion is replaced with a more communal preoccupation with humanity as a whole. For when God is understood as the personification of human nature, then who God is becomes common to all human beings and love is shared with all.[26] We might say, then, that Feuerbach's reinterpretation of Christianity "secularizes" religion so it can be of better secular use. As he once put it, "I deny only in order to affirm. I deny the fantastic projection of theology and religion in order to affirm the real essence of man."[27]

This concern to tell the truth about religion in order to help the collective human condition is clearly in the spirit of Karl Marx and Frederick Engels, though perhaps not so much in line with the individualism of the Millennial generation and the Nones. But the similarities between Feuerbach and Marx are no surprise since Marx and Engels pretty much adopted his views on religion. Engels spoke of the "liberating effect" of Feuerbach's work, how he and his Marxist colleagues had all become Feuerbachians. For Marx, Feuerbach was like a second Martin Luther in liberating people.[28]

Feuerbach, then, does not seem to have been an evil man in his intentions, a nihilist with only destructive purposes. He merely aimed to be a truth-teller for the good of the human species. He had nothing personally to gain by the positions he took. They basically torpedoed his academic career in this nineteenth-century

25. Feuerbach, *Die Philosophie der Zukunft*, 14.

26. Feuerbach, *The Essence of Christianity*, 247ff.

27. Feuerbach, *Das Wesen der Religion*, 14.

28. Engels, *Ludwig Feuerbach and the Outcome of Classical German Philosophy*, 18; Marx, "Contribution to the Critique of Hegel's Philosophy of Law," 182.

German context. But he was a good and careful scholar, who had really understood well the implications of the theology of his day. His commitment to truth led him to revise his thinking somewhat later in his 1848 lectures on "The Essence of Religion." In this work Feuerbach finds the source of religion to be human dependence on nature, on the human need to make nature less mysterious by attributing a personhood like our own on it. This is really not so different from the subjectivizing of religion, rendering it anthropology, that he posited in his earlier critique of Christianity that we have been examining. In fact, even in the earlier work on Christianity Feuerbach alluded to how religion helps us make sense of nature.[29] Consequently it seems fair to focus our interest on what Feuerbach says in his book on Christianity, especially since it was the work of Feuerbach that most occupied both Karl Marx and Karl Barth, the theologian from whom we are seeking guidance in this volume as to how to get American Christianity out of its funk. Indeed, Barth advises us that we keep Feuerbach's work on Christianity before us when we are theologizing and doing ministry. Let's see why.

KARL BARTH'S CRITIQUE

Barth's primary reason for urging us to consider Feuerbach was that the great philosopher had posed an important question for the theology of his day: whether these approaches share with Feuerbach a common methodological starting point in studying Christianity. If they do, then it seems that the theology of Feuerbach's day would inadvertently endorse his conclusion that theology is anthropology. And if the theologians of his day failed to see this or failed to make a case that their theologies do not lapse into his conclusion, the same set of questions must be posed to those who followed in the twentieth century and even up to our

---

29. Feuerbach, *Das Wesen der Religion*; Feuerbach, *The Essence of Christianity*, 189–201. For this assessment of the similarities in his thought throughout his career, also see Gerrish, "Feuerbach's Religious Illusion." Also see Harvey, *Feuerbach and the Interpretation of Religion*.

present day. Barth would have us keep using Feuerbach's critique and the ability of theologians of our day to dialogue with it as a measure of a theological approach's adequacy. (His earliest critique of Feuerbach had accused the philosopher of an unrealistic view of human nature, but as we'll see he continued to make this point along with the methodological critiques of the theology of his day on which we focus.) Barth also suggested that we study Feuerbach to clarify the vulnerability of Martin Luther and his heirs to Feuerbach's critique. (No need to explore that issue in this book, since Barth's critique failed to take into account the full richness of Luther's theology that I made clear in a recent book, and also because Lutherans employing the method Barth and I evolve will be protected from the Feuerbachian critique.)[30]

In his own constructive work in his multivolume *Church Dogmatics*, Barth stops to point out a number of issues that, a theologian's failure properly to address, will lead to capitulation to Feuerbach's reduction of Christian faith to mere human experience. Let's review these points now, trying to determine whether the dominant models for theology and ministry in our day fall short on these commitments. This will also give us a chance to determine whether Barth is correct, that errors on these points do fall prey to the Feuerbachian critique. It is my contention that Barth did not offer unequivocally successful arguments justifying his allegations on all of these issues. That may be part of the reason his warnings have been largely ignored. If I can do a good enough job now of making the case for Barth's conclusions, it may be harder for you, the guild of theologians, pastors, and mainline denominational offices to keep dodging these critiques.

Another agenda we want to consider are Barth's proposals for dealing with each of these issues. This will allow us to evaluate

30. Barth, "An Introductory Essay," xixff., xxviii–xxix. I am stressing here the continuity in Barth's various engagements with Feuerbach, contrary to the contentions of Glasse, "Barth on Feuerbach." For indications that Feuerbach himself spoke of theology becoming anthropology, see his *Das Wesen des Christentums*, 38 (English translation: *The Essence of Christianity*, 14). For my defense of Luther from Feuerbach's critique, see my *Martin Luther's Legacy*, esp. 32, 61.

whether Barth has succeeded in avoiding Feuerbach's contentions on these matters. If so, then Barth's advice might be what we need to heed in order to help revive our churches and get them out of the present slump. Let's see.

Barth contends that we begin to fall prey to Feuerbach's critique of religion—to make the human subject the creator of his determination by God—when we root our theology in a foundationalism (making faith's plausibility dependent on its being rooted in another plausible system), when we make the experience of God's Word a possibility that can be presupposed as a predicate or property of human nature or human experience.[31] It makes no difference if you start with the father of modern liberal theology, Friedrich Schleiermacher, who roots theology in human emotions; move to Paul Tillich, who finds the experience of God's Word to be rooted in our essence; consider much modern pastoral care theology, which roots faith-claims in the latest definition of psychologically healthy behavior; or move to Paul Ricoeur as well as much story preaching and mainline Bible study materials, which relate God's Word to our "story," our storytelling, narrative capacities. Even the previously noted thoughtful effort by Lutheran practical theologian Nathan Frambach to articulate a model for reaching the Nones through informal communities (the so-called Emerging Church movement), so commendable in advocating for identification with the Bible's stories, operates with these suppositions. Unfortunately all of these models for theology and ministry root Christian faith in human experience.[32]

31. Barth, *Church Dogmatics*, I/1:240–41.

32. Schleiermacher, *Christian Faith*, 4, 15–16; Tillich, *Systematic Theology*, vol. 1, 79ff.; Ricoeur, *Time and Narrative*, vol. 2, 29–60, 156–60; Buttrick, *Homiletic: Moves and Structure*, 10–11, 113, 116, 118, 259, 261, 269–70, 278–80, 321–23, 333–63; Howe, *Man's Need & God's Action*, 10ff; Frambach, *Emerging Ministry*, 36ff. For the intellectual roots of mainline church educational promotion of integrating God's Story with our stories, see Brown, "My Story and 'The Story,'" 166–73. Frei, "Remarks in Connection with a Theological Proposal," 27, has characterized modern theology as anthropocentric. Lindbeck, *Nature of Doctrine*, esp. 31, refers to the prevailing approach to theology as an Experiential-Expressive Model, since on its grounds theological statements are expressions of core religious/social experience.

Do these approaches forfeit the otherness or transcendence of God? Of course they do not intend this. But logically, if you seek to assert God's transcendence, assert that God is more than your experience, then according to the definitions of these theologians such a theological statement is merely an expression of your feelings (Schleiermacher and much pastoral care theology), a symbolic expression of the depth of reason (Tillich), or an expression of creative storytelling (Ricoeur and Frambach). It is true that Paul Ricoeur does protest this identification with Feuerbach on grounds that he does not have consciousness posit itself, for in his view self-understanding is replying to the biblical text.[33] But he does not address the charge that his theological statements are themselves rooted in the narrative character of history and our experience of it which he posits.

An earlier attempt to respond to Feuerbach in the mid-1970s was offered by Edward Farley. Relying on Edmund Husserl and phenomenology, in the spirit of Ricoeur, he posits that transcendental consciousness reflects the structures of the world, so that religious assertions emerging from our transcendental consciousness are not just expressions of subjectivity. Others can perceive what I am perceiving. It is just common sense, then, that phenomenology could account for Feuerbach's critique of religion. But in fact the starting point for Farley and phenomenology for perceiving the structures of the life-world and intersubjective objects to which Christian faith refers is not these structures and objects themselves but our perception of them.[34] Similarly, famed Catholic theologian Karl Rahner offers an argument for the reality of Christianity on grounds that grace is the foundation of knowing grace, for grace is said to permeate the human experience. But he still contends that theology must be anthropology, that grace subsists in human experience. Another famous Catholic theologian, Bernard Lonergan, makes a similar point in claiming that true objectivity is the

33. Ricoeur, *Essays on Biblical Interpretation*, 109; Ricoeur, *Interpretation Theory*, 93.

34. Farley, *Ecclesial Man*, esp. 7, 9, 43–45, 128–30.

fruit of authentic subjectivity.[35] And so for Farley, Lonergan, and Rahner as well as well as another well-known Catholic theologian Edward Schillebeeckx, what we perceive about Christianity is ultimately rooted in our perceptions or creative discoveries, not in the Word that precedes our experience of it.[36] The Word cannot stand alone on their grounds, and so it is not clear how God's Word and the things of God are more than a projection of human experience. Feuerbach's critique of religion is not refuted, an effective alternative to it not offered. These same problems also plague much constructive, feminist, and even liberation theology as we'll note in the next chapter.[37]

Karl Barth addresses this set of problems raised by the rooting of transubjective realities in our perception of them quite clearly by insisting that it is the Word of God that creates the possibility of experiencing it, that normative understandings of Scripture and theology, not dependent on the interpreter's experience, are possible.[38] When everything about revelation, even our ability to understand it, is initiated by God, there is no way that any one speaking of this revelation can be heard as something people are making up. Armed with a Barthian point of view, to anyone challenging Christian claims as just someone's opinion, the response is, "No way it's my thinking. On my own I couldn't even come up with an idea like what I'm telling you."

The next thing that Barth says we need to avoid in our ministries if we want to avoid the specter of subjectivism and relativism is to make it clear that we have not initiated our theological reflection with human experience.[39] Schleiermacher, Tillich, and

35. Rahner, *Theological Investigations*, vol. 9, 28ff. Lonergan, *Method in Theology*, 112–13, 156–58, 392.

36. Schillebeeckx, *Jesus*, esp. 61–62.

37. Alves, *A Theology of Human Hope*, 4–5, 72–74, 165–66; Daly, *Beyond God the Father*, 6ff. An analysis of Constructive Theology suppositions that exhibit these problems is offered by a proponent of this approach, Wyman, *Constructing Constructive Theology*, esp. 172. For James Cone, see the next chapter.

38. Barth, *Church Dogmatics*, I/1:239–40.

39. Barth, *Church Dogmatics*, I/1:144–45.

prominent pastoral care theologians do this when they root the possibility of revelation in experience. In addition, we need to consider how at times in his career James Cone, the founder of Black Theology, as well as much Feminist Theology (Rosemary Radford Ruether) operate this way.[40] A lot of denominational educational literature is rooted in educational theory. Once again, if we begin our theology with human experience, then everything we say theologically speaking, even denials that revelation is not rooted in human experience, must logically be an expression of human experience. Start with experience in your theology and you never escape it, never hear the voice of the transcendent God. No wonder Western mainline churches are intuitively perceived by many as not being spiritual enough, as too worldly. In buying into this theological and educational model, everything they do and say seems to be about the world, not about God and his Word.

Barth responds very clearly to this abuse. He insists that the Word of God "must no longer appear as conditioned by this investigation [of anthropology], must cease to show itself anywhere near a 'proper anthropology'; it must be evolved prior to and independently of the latter."[41] Armed with this insight, Christians will not be so easily seen as merely proposing a remedy to today's needs. In fact, the response to skeptics from the Barthian viewpoint is that we do not even know who we are and what our problems are apart from God's Word. God tells us who we are and what we need. This might be a powerful Word for a people so caught up in the multitude of options that we are losing our way.

Barth also warns that we fall prey to Feuerbach's critique of religion as nothing more than a description of what the human species wants when the possibility of God's freedom and revelation is first posited as an ontological reality before affirming the

40. Cone, *Black Theology and Black Power*; Ruether, *Sexism and God-Talk*, 12. For leaders in the development of pastoral care theology who employed this model, see Wise, *The Meaning of Pastoral Care*, esp. 20ff.; Howe, *Man's Need & God's Action*, 14–15, 115. Also see footnote 32 above.

41. Barth, *Church Dogmatics*, I/1:144–45.

actuality of revelation.[42] Ludwig Feuerbach himself seemed to endorse Barth's way of seeking to overcome reduction of Christian claims to anthropology. Thus the great philosopher claimed that "a God Who gives me a knowledge of Himself through His own act is alone a God Who truly exists, who proves Himself to exist,—an objective God."[43]

There are indeed significant theological approaches that embody this tendency. The Process Philosophy conceptuality employed by Process theologians John Cobb and David Griffin does not allow them to assert God's sovereignty over world events (since on Process grounds God only sends out lures that may or may not affect behavior). Consequently, God is only known when we respond to his love. Our experience is a necessary ingredient in revelation. And Paul Tillich's insistence that revelation is rooted in the depth of reason, that God works through his creatures, entails that a God who is not impacted by our trials is impossible.[44] God is not working independently of us on these grounds. Indeed, theological statements about his work have been shaped by our philosophical constructs. And as we have noted, when human constructs shape what we say of God, then the concept of God and his work never stands over against us as a transcendent reality. And in that case, everything we say, theologically speaking, even denials that revelation is rooted in human experience, must logically be an expression of human experience. Put God and his work in your philosophical box, then you never escape that human box into which you have put God, never hear the voice of transcendent God. But when revelation comes to us prior to developing an interpretive framework, then its words shape us. We cannot impose our "human meaning/experience" on this revelation!

Maybe the reason that the public does not seem so interested in God is that we have so "humanized" him. He is no longer a God bigger than we are, not as likely to command our respect. In

42. Barth, *Church Dogmatics*, I/2:4–6.

43. Feuerbach, *The Essence of Christianity*, 204.

44. Cobb and Griffin, *Process Theology*, 43, 96–97; Tillich, *Systematic Theology*, vol. 1, 83–86, 264ff.

fact, a 2018 Pew Research Center poll revealed that just 62 percent of mainline Protestants (only 33 percent of all American college graduates) believe God is all-powerful, that he has the power to change everything.[45] Yes, God has been trivialized, perhaps because our prevailing theologies in mainline Christianity and in its schools have presented God in ways that trivialize, humanize the deity. What Barth does to make God's transcendence clear is to insist that our personhood is not divine in nature, but a contradiction of the divine nature. As he puts it (in a way that contradicts much of the Nones' identification of the self with God but may still allure them by this vision of a great God): "It [Holy Scripture] also assumes that God is in no way bound to man, that His revelation is thus an act of His freedom, contradicting man's contradiction."[46]

Then Barth reminds us that we can only do this by making sure that theology is distinguished from all philosophy and historical science of religion.[47] This is a message for the academy and denominational offices. Don't systematically mix what you say about faith with other worldviews (be they online connectedness, philosophies of self-respect, or the latest politically correct value), or you might end up trivializing God and the things of the church.

Barth's next warning about how to avoid the Feuerbachian consequence of reducing Christian faith to human experience is in line with the preceding warning. The great theologian warns us that if Christianity is dealt with as just another human religion there is room only for natural religion as the illusory expression of the natural longings and wishes of the human heart.[48]

The academy is replete with this tendency to relate Christianity to other religions, to regard Christianity as another religion. Thus undergraduate Christian institutions now typically have religion (not theology or Christian studies) departments in which Christianity is studied, and religion is presented as a set of

45. Pew Research Center, "When Americans Say They Believe in God, What Do They Mean?"

46. Barth, *Church Dogmatics*, I/2:7.

47. Barth, *Church Dogmatics*, I/2:7.

48. Barth, *Church Dogmatics*, I/2:289–90.

human activities and beliefs. Among important theologians equating Christianity with other religions are Paul Tillich and African scholar John Mbiti.[49] The impact of these dynamics appears in a recent document of the Evangelical Lutheran Church in America, "A Declaration of Our Inter-religious Commitment." The document does not advocate evangelism of those of other religions and defines faith as "trust" with the understanding that faith is not about affirming beliefs.[50] Obviously, then, America's largest Lutheran body seems open to contending that the faith of Jews and Muslims is like its own members' faith!

In a society saturated by Feuerbachian thinking, even if we do not realize it, everything concerning religion is about human experience and activity. That is why we can refer to Christianity and other religions as about faith, no matter what their revelations. The attitudes reflected in the Lutheran document are also reflected in the polls. A 2014 Pew Research Center poll found that 66 percent of American Christians believe that many religions can lead to eternal life (only 29 percent of us believing that salvation comes only through their religion).[51]

Feuerbach's critique of the theology of his day certainly seems to apply to today. Interpret Christianity as just another religion, in light of human categories, and you start presenting it as something humans do. Karl Barth tries to overcome these dynamics again by focusing on God's revelation without imposing our own human interpretive schemes on what is revealed in Christ. He does this by contending that God's revelation is "the abolition of religion." For religion is a human phenomenon, Barth insists! It is something you can grasp historically and psychologically. In fact, the revelation in Jesus Christ teaches us that religion is false![52] If we want a theology that does not fall prey to the Feuerbachian reduction of

---

49. Mbiti, "The Encounter of Christian Faith and African Religion"; Tillich, *Systematic Theology*, vol. 1, 215–16, 219–20.

50. Evangelical Lutheran Church in America, "A Declaration of Our Inter-religious Commitments."

51. Pew Research Center, "Importance of Religion and Religious Beliefs."

52. Barth, *Church Dogmatics*, I/2:280, 281, 297ff.

religion to a human activity, we must make sure that the uniqueness of Christian faith is stressed. The fact that it is institutionally and culturally difficult to make that case in our present mainline church ethos indicates how careful and countercultural we will need to be in developing our theologies if we want to avoid the consequences of seeming to present Christianity as just another option.

Barth's next warning about how to avoid Feuerbach's critique is to advise us to not just focus on the benefits of Christ, rather than Christ himself. In the same vein, he noted that we also unwittingly endorse Feuerbach when we speak of the church ascribing titles to Jesus and do not passively confess that he has fully revealed himself.[53]

The idea of a passive confession is of course no longer fashionable in theological circles since Kant and the idea that all our knowledge is a function of the interpreter's experience of it. All of the theologians we have noted thus far in this section subscribe to this supposition. But theologians still exerting an impact to this very day subscribe to the idea that the faithful are the ones who have identified who Christ is, who have ascribed titles to him. Perhaps the most famous living theologian falling prey to this critique is Jürgen Moltmann. He calls for us to interpret all that Christ does and is in light of the eschaton.[54] It is also fascinating to note that

---

53. Barth, *Church Dogmatics*, IV/3.2, 563–64; Barth, *Church Dogmatics*, IV/3.1, 69–74. It should be noted that Barth is to some extent critiquing Martin Luther and his heritage at this point, since Luther is known to have at times stressed the benefits of Christ's Work, the importance of faith "for me" (*pro me*). See Luther, *Commentary on Galatians*, 299. But Luther also combines this focus on Christ's benefits for us with an insistence that what he has done is for all the elect; *Lectures on Romans*, 370. Elsewhere, when just explicating the faith, the Reformer makes even clearer that his focus is Christ and what he has done, not just its benefits to the faithful. See *The Eighteenth and Nineteenth Chapters of John*, 406; cf. 219ff. Feuerbach might also criticize Luther for his definition of God as the object of one's whole-hearted trust (Luther, *The Large Catechism*, 133). But in many cases, when not dealing with issues of how to live as a Christian, the Reformer clearly articulates God's essence (see *Confession Concerning Christ's Supper*, 339).

54. Moltmann, *Theology of Hope*, 202–3.

a number of the most influential mainline theology textbooks of our century have been produced by the school of Constructive Theology, whose proponents stress the creative character of our interpretation of biblical symbols.[55]

Indeed, hang around biblical studies departments in most mainline educational institutions, and you'll find that virtually all the New Testament faculty members will tell you that the church conferred on Jesus his titles, that he never saw himself as Messiah, divine, and the like. Little wonder that many seminary graduates find themselves not reading the Bible for spiritual edification after graduating. What we say about Jesus in the church is widely seen as titles conferred on him by the church, by human beings, just ways of trying to understand him. No surprise, then, that according to Barna Group's most recent poll on the subject in 2015 just 56 percent of American Christians and an even more alarming only 22 percent in England believe Jesus is divine.[56]

Barth says that if this is what we do then we are just joining Ludwig Feuerbach in making Jesus and God in our own image. And we have no competence for judging Jesus, but we can hear his living voice (in the Word).[57] Again it is just a matter of starting our theologizing with the actuality of God's revelation!

Barth offers one other way to respond to Feuerbach. We need to recognize, he says, that "even in our relation to God, we are and remain liars, and that we can lay claim to His truth, His certainty, His salvation as *grace* and *only* as grace."[58] This observation stems from Barth's appreciation of the optimistic views of human nature that prevailed in the theology of Feuerbach's day. Feuerbach himself had clearly appropriated this optimistic thinking.[59]

---

55. Wyman, *Constructing Constructive Theology*, esp. 25, 167; S. Jones, *Feminist Theory and Christian Theology*, vii, claims she is just mapping links from biblical images to our context.

56. Barna Research, "What Do Americans Believe about Jesus? 5 Popular Beliefs"; Barna Research, "Perception of Jesus, Christians & Evangelism in the UK."

57. Barth, *Church Dogmatics*, IV/3.1, 72ff.

58. Barth, "An Introductory Essay," xxix.

59. For this assessment, see Barth, *Protestant Thought: From Roussseau to*

Not much has changed since Feuerbach's time. An optimism about human nature continues to prevail in mainline theology. Good examples may be seen in an early feminist theologian, Georgia Harkness. And in Liberation Theology, though it is common to refer to social sin and the fallen character of unjust structures, there is no discussion by many of these theologians of the sinfulness of the oppressed.[60] Most of the time in seminary pastoral care departments we hear a lot of talk about the need to boost self-esteem. Hardly surprising in view of the prevalence of these values in society and Peter Berger's appreciation of the fact that the more the churches struggle with secularization the more they are likely to adopt the latest social trends.

Poll data bears out the influence of these trends on American attitudes. A 2018 poll conducted by LifeWay Research found that over three in four Americans (77 percent) reject the idea that God will punish people for small sins. No reason to fear this since 66 percent of us think people are essentially good![61]

The God-man who is Feuerbach's ideal, the human being, who has learned that God is the ideal of what humans can become here and now, is no longer so preoccupied with life after death. This is why those who share an optimism about human nature will not be so focused on the grace of God. They will be more focused on what humans must do and experience. But if I know that because of sin I can never do this, that only by the gift of grace can I hope to see this happen, then my theology will focus more on an external God and less on human activity.

Barth reminds us that if we want to put to rest the idea that religion is about what humans do—if we want to get the church out of its funk—we need to get more real about human nature and our need for God's grace.

Ritschl, 360–61.

60. Harkness, *Understanding the Christian Faith,* 16–23, 114–20; Alves, *Theology of Human Hope,* 106ff.

61. LifeWay Research, "2018 State of American Theology Study Research Report."

CONCLUSION: NEXT STEPS

With this analysis complete, it seems that we could end the book. We have identified how many of the characteristics of the prevailing styles of theology and ministry in mainline American and European Christianity fall prey to the critique made of Christianity by Feuerbach. Little wonder, then, in view of how embedded Feuerbach's subjectivism and human-centered way of thinking are in Western society (Freud and our therapeutic consciousness have taught us to regard religion as just a way of meeting human needs) that the teaching and preaching of mainline Christianity have come to be dismissed by the public.[62]

Notre Dame historian James Turner nicely explains why the compromise of transcendence by the dominant theologians of our day matters and what its consequences have been. He wrote,

> God's purposes were not supposed to be man's. . . . They forgot, in short, that their God was . . . radically other than man. . . . Unbelief emerged because church leaders too often forgot the transcendence essential to any worthwhile God. They committed religion *functionally* to making the world better in human terms and *intellectually* to modes of knowing God fitted only for understanding the world.[63]

Another analyst of the Nones, Linda Mercandante, makes a related point regarding how the mainline churches have failed, unwittingly contributing to the growth of the Nones by "adapting to the contemporary world all too well."[64] They have unwittingly buried the essence of faith, downplaying the awe we should feel in God's presence.

Of course, most church leaders have not heard about Feuerbach and his critiques of Christianity, and don't really address the

---

62. On the impact of Freud's view of religion as wish fulfillment on contemporary attitudes, see Aslan, *God: A Human History*, esp. 32–33; Mercadante, *Belief without Borders*, 128–29, 142, 154.

63. Turner, *Without God, Without Creed*, xii, 266–67.

64. Mercadante, *Belief without Borders*, 251.

skepticism toward religion as something made up by humans that prevails in pop culture. Besides, today's church leaders don't have a theology that makes clear that Christian teachings are more than human wish fulfillment. That's a primary reason why the churches in the West are in the mess they are in. But now with Barth's critique of Feuerbach we have some handles for overcoming these trends. It's time we get away from starting with human experience, with trying to root faith in contemporary experience and social currents, with optimistic understandings of how good and decent we are, instead of making clear that God's work and the Bible stories are what tell us who we are (and that we're not as good as we think we are). The book's finished! Now we know how to get the churches out of their funk!

Not so fast. Barth's positions were articulated well before the decline of mainline Christianity began in the 1960s. We need another chapter to explain why his critique of Feuerbach and associated proposals never did catch fire; we need to examine the problems with his proposals. We'll see that an awful lot of church leaders think that a focus on the literal Word of God is not going to attract postmodern people, that Barth's proposals will not present a relevant version of the Word. We need to start our preaching and teaching with our context and experience, these voices cry. We also need to explain why things have even gotten worse and why the mainline theological establishment has done so little to engage and critique Feuerbach's analysis.

Then in the final chapter, I will try to plug the holes in Barth's proposal, highlight points in his thought most have missed, and show how this emerging proposal can link with the best in these segments of Western Christianity still holding the line against the relativizing of faith to which most mainline church leaders have capitulated. I will then show how a theology based broadly on his orientation can be presented to the public as intellectually attractive, as "scientifically sound" proposals. Though you already have much of what you need to stem the currents that are lousing up Western Christianity, the next chapters are for those who need more convincing.

4

The State of Barth and His Critique Today

The Conspiracy of Silence in the Classroom,
Headquarters, and Pulpit, and Why It Matters

The convincing character of Feuerbach's critique of Christianity and its pertinence to the way in which most theology is done in the modern world, pertinence to how American and Western European mainline church leaders function, should now be readily apparent to open-minded readers. There is no logical escape from the conclusions, is there? If theology is constructed in such a way that all statements about Christianity are necessarily related to human experience or our context, such that there is nothing we can say about faith whose meaning stands independent of human experience, then everything Christian is ultimately about human experience. No reality claimed by Christians clearly transcends human experience. Even to claim that God transcends experience is just an assertion of human experience. The overwhelming logic of this argument seems irrefutable. I have been struggling with it since first exposed to it as a college junior. If readers can shoot it down and demonstrate how theologies correlating the Word of God with human experience can counter this logic, I will be happy to see it. But in fifty years of study I have yet to see such an argument. In fact, in the academy there has existed what seems to be something like a "conspiracy of silence" about the force of Feuerbach's critique of Christianity (sort of like the neglect of the points I made about mainline church life in the second chapter).

How come? Why this failure to consider Feuerbach's critique? In a sense we've already answered that one. The mainline denominations and the theological establishments as a whole have too much invested in their commitments to theologies connecting the Word to personal experience and our cultural context. It's all about the quest for "relevance." After the 1970s, if not before, relevance began to be defined as inclinations to address women's issues, gay liberation, and even a little ecology; or, in the case of the Prosperity Gospel, it was about being relevant to economic themes. And any theological position that does not aim for relevance in accord with the prevailing models will be dismissed as "irrelevant."

There has been another side effect of this passion for relevancy. With the possible exception of the prosperity gospel and a concern with economic success, the issues defined as relevant in the academy and mainline church offices are largely white-collar professional concerns, a function of the lack of presence of blue-collar representation in mainline denominational offices and the committees the white-collar staff convene. Gay rights, ecology, multiculturalism, and creative control are not the issues of the working family, exhausted from a hard day's work, worried about job security and retirement, and discontent with life as a result of the tension observed between what's on the screen and everyday life in the neighborhood, factory, or office. Mainline denominations are no longer churches of the people in their programming, resourcing, and training of clergy. This explains 2016 poll data that indicate that among the Nones, 53 percent have only a high-school education or less (while a minority, 46 percent, have a college degree). An earlier General Social Survey has found that blue-collar white workers are far more likely than white workers with professional positions (59 percent to 41 percent) to be de facto secularists, and that since the 1970s there was a 20 percent gap between blue-collar white and white professionals in church arttendance.[1] The differences in these polls suggest that the failure to attract blue-collar Americans pertains more to whites than African-American and Hispanic laborers. No two ways about it: strategies of "relevance" by mainline churches and the theological establishment are not working for the white working class.

The best way to proceed for the theological academy and the mainline denominational officials has been to ignore the problems that these dynamics cause. Don't address Feuerbach or engage Karl Barth's response to theologies vulnerable to his critique. (Also, under the guise of getting the "best" laity on your church-wide committees, don't worry about looking for blue-collar, working-class representation.) I am not naïve. The challenges issued to the academy and the denominations that this book raises may experience the same fate as Feuerbach's critique of Christianity has. But sadly, this neglect will just vindicate the arguments I've been making too. The failure of the mainline denominations considered in this study systematically to address the growth of the Nones is one indication that the issues raised in this book may not get on the radar screen in the various headquarters. And the theological points I've been making will step on the toes of a lot of sacred cows in the academy and in mainline seminaries.

That's awfully pessimistic. People still read Barth, and there have been some articles or books which include attention to Feuerbach's critique in recent years. Part of the reason for my pessimism is that since the 1960s and with each passing decade the situation I've described in the previous chapter has even gotten worse.

Since the 1960s Barth's theology has fallen on hard times. The growing secularism has taken a toll. The lumping together of him with Emil Brunner, Reinhold Niebuhr, Paul Tillich, and Rudolf Bultmann in the genre of Neo-Orthodoxy reflected how even in the years of his greatest popularity relatively little attention in the academy had been paid to his dialogue with Feuerbach. For the

1. Pew Research Center, "Educational Attainment among the Religiously Unaffiliated"; for data on the General Social Survey poll, see Murray, *Coming Apart*, 202ff. For prosperity gospel suppositions, see Osteen, *Your Best Life Now*, 82ff.; Copeland, *Prosperity*, esp. 11–12.

Feuerbachian critique pertains to Tillich (as we have already observed) and also to Bultmann, if not Brunner.[2] And so it made no sense to lump Barth with these other theologians if you have his critique of Feuerbach in view.

Most observers agree that, even in denominations whose seminaries in the golden years of the Neo-Orthodox movement had focused on this theological approach and the associated Biblical Theology Movement advocated by scholars like G. Ernest Wright and Floyd Filson, these efforts to ground theology in the Bible's literal sense and in Reformation categories never had that much of an impact on the American and Western European pews or in the pop culture of these nations.[3] The very fact that these movements never were embraced in a widespread way in fundamentalist or even evangelical circles entails that they should have functioned as a third way between the fundamentalist-modernist divide.[4] But there seems to be little awareness of this in American pop culture. Barth's and Neo-Orthodoxy's failure to influence pop culture is evident in the way polls are conducted to this day. Those polled never get a chance to qualify whether they believe a middle ground between the Bible being the actual Word of God taken literally or not to be taken literally.[5] The fundamentalist or liberal

2. See above, 45–46, 49, for the critique of Tillich. For Bultmann's grounding of the Word of God in experience, see his *Jesus Christ and Mythology*, 18, 45, 48, 51. For Brunner's commitment to relating the Word and experience, see his *Offenbarung und Vernunft*, esp. 65.

3. Childs, *Biblical Theology in Crisis*, 59–60, notes how little indication there is in sermons during the golden age of these movements in America that Biblical Theology is playing much of a role in influencing these sermons. And if not in the sermons, there would be little likelihood of Neo-Orthodox influence on church life prior to 1970.

4. An early, influential critique of Barth in evangelical circles was offered by Van Til, *The New Modernism*. See the most eminent evangelical theologian of the last century Carl F. H. Henry, *God, Revelation, and Authority*, vol. 4, esp. 196–200. More recent evangelicals express a bit more friendliness toward Barth. See McCormack and Anderson, *Karl Barth and American Evangelicalism*. Save perhaps for Princeton Seminary, Barth's influence may be more evident today in American evangelical circles than anywhere else in American Christianity.

5. An example of such polling options is evident in Saad, "Three in Four in

options are still the only shows in town for the average American. Nobody but older theological scholars, not even many pastors, knows about Neo-Orthodoxy.

Since the cultural revolutions of the 1960s, a growing sense that Barth did not address the pressing issues of the day (liberation, poverty, women's issues) emerged. (This is perhaps a bogus critique when one considers his liberal social ethic, his socialist orientation, and his standing up to the Nazis.) But a substantive issue that has probably most led to a retreat of support was his concept of the Bible as salvation-history (the distinction he made between ordinary history accessible to the critical historian [*Historie*] and the reality in which God appears and works in history [*Geschichte*] only accessible in faith).[6] Arguments have been made against the intellectual honesty of this distinction. It seems dishonest to claim that something is historical when it violates the rules of what can be deemed historical, since on Barth's grounds these realities cannot be perceived by ordinary historical means. It would be a bit like a smitten teenager contending that an attractive member of the opposite sex had declared his or her passionate love for the teen simply on the basis of the teen's interpretation of some alleged smile, wink, or act of kindness offered by the other.[7]

The seriousness of this problem led to the development at Yale University of the so-called postliberal approach. My own proposal in the next chapter tries to employ Barth in a way that avoids these problems as well. But nonetheless, except perhaps for the theological faculties of Princeton Theological Seminary, Duke Divinity School, and a handful of other seminaries, the comments of Matthew Rose, who in 2014 claimed that Barth's work "is today a dead letter," seem vindicated. Evangelicals influenced by Barth are retiring.[8] Schools that had something like Barth's perspective at

---

U.S. Still See the Bible as Word of God."

6. Barth, *Church Dogmatics*, I/1:373–78; IV/1:333–37.

7. For such critiques, see Childs, *Biblical Theology in Crisis*, 62ff.; Harvey, *The Historian & the Believer*, 153–59.

8. Rose, "Karl Barth's Failure." For a discussion of the impact of Barth on several now-aging evangelicals of the last century, see Lewis, *Karl Barth in North America*.

the forefront of their pedagogy even in the 1990s (institutions like Columbia Seminary in Decatur, Georgia, and most of the Evangelical Lutheran Church in America seminaries) have recruited faculty in theology more preoccupied with liberation, feminist, or womanist approaches. Thus they have adopted theological profiles more in the line with the dominant models of theology described in the previous chapters (the commitments to grounding the affirmations of faith in human experience or some foundational ontology).

The general neglect of Barth that Rose, Childs, and I observe here will be objected to by some associated with Princeton. It is true that a significant number of books about Barth and his theology continue to be published. But it is significant that in the twenty-first century not one article on Barth has appeared in the cutting-edge journal of the American Academy of Religion. His name is rarely mentioned in the twenty-first century in *The Christian Century*, the cutting-edge theological journal of American Lutheranism, *Dialog*, or even in the prestigious journal *Theology Today*.

An admirer of Barth, George Lindbeck, provides another account of this neglect of Barth as a resource for cutting-edge theology. By claiming that the actuality of God's Word overcomes our subjectivity in interpretation, Barth is diminishing the interpreter's role in determining meaning. (He has to do that in order to overcome Feuerbach's critique.) But, as Lindbeck notes, this commitment flies in the face of the ethos of our time. For our era, he contends, is an age that stresses authenticity, self-expression as the highest good. That's why theological perspectives stressing the interpreter's role in determining the meaning of the Word of God are so popular today.[9] And on that score, then, Barth is not in fashion.

This observation is borne out by the analysis of several theologians of this century analyzing the development of Postliberal Theology that grew out of Barth's insights and was developed by Lindbeck and other Yale colleagues in the last decades of the twentieth century. A number of theological works were generated by

9. Lindbeck, *Nature of Doctrine*, 23.

this approach, and among those thought to be associated with it is the scholar named "America's best theologian" in 2001 by *Time* magazine, Stanley Hauerwas. This postliberal approach will influence the next chapter. However, a book has been written about this Barthian-influenced approach's decline![10] Writing some years earlier than this book pronouncing the movement's demise, another scholar, Gary Dorrien, observed that although in its earliest stages proponents of this approach were Barthian, in the sense of seeking to conserve tradition, in contrast to University of Chicago theological liberalism, "Today the advocates of Yale postliberalism and Chicago liberalism are probably outnumbered by those who, like [Kathryn] Tanner, are trying to build bridges between these approaches."[11] A theology committed to the objective reality of the Word of God, standing over against us and our experience, overcoming our subjectivity, is pronounced as dead or outnumbered by the alternatives.

Other examples of the silencing of a commitment to a theology that does not involve the interpreter's constructive contribution to a text's meaning can be readily provided. You silence the critique by claiming a middle-ground position between this alternative and relativism. But such a middle-ground position logically does not exist. Consider as an excellent example an anonymous reader's feedback to a proposed article negating the interpreter's role in determining a text's meaning for the guild's cutting-edge theological journal, *Theology Today*. The anonymous critic writes,

> It [the article] sees only relativism and realism or objectivism as alternatives and lacks the sophistication of any form of critical realism. It presumes that a constructive role for the interpreter in determining meaning equals the complete determination of meaning by the constructions of the interpreter. It does not understand that a role need not be a sole role. It lacks the sophistication to see that the role of the interpreter, and the whole Kantian

---

10. DeHart, *The Trial of Witnesses.*
11. Dorrien, "The Future of Postliberal Theology," 22–29.

> turn to the subject, might condition but not determine
> the understanding of truth.

Apparently, these commitments reflect the editorial policies of this prestigious journal. Let's examine them.

It seems to makes sense to concede the supposition that in conditioning the meaning of a text the interpreter might not *totally* distort the text's literal meaning. But as I shall point out in the next chapter with reference to modern physics (the principle of uncertainty of Werner Heisenberg) that supposition is fallacious. At any rate, at this point ordinary logic indicates that as soon as we inject human experience into the equation of determining a text's meaning, or have it play a material role in determining its meaning (no matter how little a role the interpreter's experience plays), that text is no longer an objective reality standing over-against us. And once that happens with biblical and other Christian affirmations, Feuerbach's critique that these statements are products of human experience cannot be refuted. For even our claims that the Word is of God, that God determines "most" of its meaning, on grounds of the anonymous critic quoted above that comment too is at least in part an expression of human experience. And who says that claim on the part of the anonymous critic is anything more than an expression of human experience? With a hermeneutic or theology like the one in operation in at least some of the judgments of one of the premier journals of the American theological establishment, Christianity cannot withstand Feuerbach's reduction of it to mere humanism.

The same theological predispositions as that of the critic cited above seem on display in Gary Dorrien's previously noted claim that most theologians want to find a middle ground between a wholehearted affirmation of the role of experience in providing a foundation for faith statements (the Chicago School) and advocates of the Word of God overcoming our subjectivity and independent of it (early Postliberal Theology). The middle ground does not exist, the logic of the preceding arguments demonstrate! As soon as you mix the Word with human experience in some way, the Word does not fully transcend you and your experience.

And then Feuerbach's critique is vindicated. If Dorrien is correct in his observations that this is the theology dominating today, is it surprising, then, that the mainline churches being informed by such a theology are in a funk? We are just preparing pastors who feed the public and our flocks a gospel watered down by options people can get from the media or learn by themselves.

The neglect of theological options, like Barth's, committed to the objective Word of God standing over against our experience along with the diminution of Barth's theology is evidenced by the widespread use of textbooks in the status seminaries that contradict his core commitments. The school of Constructive Theology, comprised of theologians teaching at many of the big-name seminaries, has produced three textbooks since the 1970s, many of which are used in these seminaries and elsewhere. The core supposition of this school of theology—that theological assertions are constructed imaginatively and creatively by human thought—embodies precisely the position that falls prey to Feuerbach's critique of Christianity.[12] Seminary students at many of our most prestigious seminaries (most American and Western European theological schools) are regularly exposed to this way of thinking as *the* way to do theology and to preach.

Even more radical versions of the commitment to a role for the interpreter in determining meaning have been developed since the 1960s. Analysts have spoken of our "surpassing" the modern era, contending that we now live in "postmodern" times. This new period is distinct from modernity insofar as truth is not objective and scientifically ascertained but is socially constructed (though scientific facts can still be obtained through methodological, disciplined inquiry).[13] Proponents of the concept are often of a nihilistic bent (a belief that all values and grand narratives [truths] are imposed on us by an oppressor, and we need to critique them

---

12. Hodgson and King, *Christian Theology*; S. Jones and Lakeland, *Constructive Theology*; Ray Jr. and Schneider, *Awake to the Moment*. For the description of the core tenets of these books, see Wyman Jr., *Constructing Constructive Theology*, esp. 175, 167.

13. Anderson, "Introduction: What's Going On Here?," 2.

as such). The widespread dominance of this way of thinking in academic circles is evidenced by NYU philosopher Paul Boghossian as he writes in the middle of the last decade:

> Over the past twenty years or so, however, a remarkable consensus has formed—in the human and social sciences, even if not in the natural sciences—around a thesis about the nature of human knowledge. It is the thesis that knowledge is socially constructed.[14]

Tied with these developments has been the emergence of a literary analytic approach termed deconstruction, an approach that posits that the use of language in a given text and language as a whole are irreducibly complex and unstable. Texts can mean whatever the powers that be want them to mean.[15] These attitudes have begun to be reflected in the thinking of some theologians. Thus Mark C. Taylor regards Christian symbols as free-floating signs, Mary Daly rejected the possibility of "unique and changeless revelation peculiar to Christianity," and Catherine Keller along with Laurel Schneider speak of the open-ended, pluralist character of religious thought, its dependence on theological creativity.[16] A school of theology known as Postcolonial Hermeneutics has begun to develop. Its proponents would put aside questions of truth in order to generate faith and hope in order to challenge oppression.[17] There is no way to refute Feuerbach's critique of Christianity on the grounds of the suppositions of these theologians. Barth's theological insights are nowhere in sight of these theological commitments now prevalent in so many American seminaries today. With such attitudes also permeating pop culture, and many pastors now provided with no resources to critique these trends, no wonder things really have gotten worse since the 1960s.

14. Boghossian, *Fear of Knowledge*, vi.

15. Derrida, *Limited Inc*, 19–21, 148–50; Derrida, *Of Grammatology*.

16. M. Taylor, "Discrediting God," 607, 623; Daly, *Beyond God the Father*, 7; Keller and Schneider, *Polydoxy Theology*, 1.

17. Punt, "Postcolonial Biblical Criticism in South Africa," 72; Syrotinski, *Deconstruction and the Postcolonial*.

WHAT'S BECOME OF FEUERBACH AND HIS CRITIQUE?

Even if you belong to the Karl Barth Society, still do your theology inspired by his insights, and so reject the preceding observations, you would surely agree that Feuerbach and Barth's critique of him are not at the forefront of the twenty-first-century academy's theological agenda. What Barth said in 1926 about his nemesis' status in the field of theology seems still true: "Rather, he [Feuerbach] is relegated to the corner seemingly the farthest removed from theology, among the sensationalists, the positivists, or even the materialists."[18] In all the books noted above about Barth, none of them devotes much if any attention to Barth's engagement with Feuerbach.

There are few incentives for scholars to take on Feuerbach's critique. To affirm its validity with regard to the dominant trends of modern theology puts the scholar against the prevailing strands and assumptions of the establishment. This could be a career-buster. It is likely harder to get published and if you do get published it becomes more likely your work gets ignored. You are also less likely to attract students if you step on some sacred cows of pop culture (which is relativistic, as we've noted) and also for many of the same reasons catch the eye of denominational officials. On top of that, you might have your scholarship impugned for sounding too much like the fundamentalists or evangelicals. (Make no mistake: though there are exceptions in some ecumenically committed segments of the theological establishment, for all the talk one hears about appreciating diversity and pluralism, evangelicals and fundamentalists will get bashed.)

It is true that at least in evangelical circles American theologians have considered Feuerbach. If this were a book for academics, I could go into great detail reviewing every one of these instances. Take a look at the footnotes if you want details. The most eminent evangelical theologian of the last century, Carl Henry, is among this number. He and most of the rest mount sound arguments in

18. Barth, "Introductory Essay," x.

support of Feuerbach's conclusions, arguing like Barth that you cannot refute the German philosopher if you do not, like Barth, assert the objectivity of God's Word, insist that its meaning is not conditioned by our experience.[19]

It may be that the arguments in these books for the pertinence of Feuerbach's critique of theologies mandating links between the Word and human experience are as strong or even stronger than mine are. But unfortunately they have been ignored by the mainline theological establishment, so maybe similar critiques by an insider like me can get some more attention. Certainly the alternative these evangelical theologians offer, relying on an inerrant Bible to dispute Feuerbach, will not fly in the mainline seminaries and their denominations. I've got a theological proposal in the next chapter that makes this book and its overall efforts to revive attention to Feuerbach's critique and respond to it in a more unique and more persuasive manner compared to these evangelical proposals, though my aim is also to propose a theological position that could be palatable in evangelical circles.

Of course, it is also not the case that mainline theologians have totally ignored Feuerbach. We have already noted how Edward Farley, Bernard Lonergan, and Karl Rahner engaged Feuerbach's criticism of Christianity in the 1970s and the reasons why their efforts were unsuccessful. But several other eminent mainline theologians like Paul Ricoeur, David Tracy, advocates of Radical Orthodoxy, Jürgen Moltmann, and Wolfhart Pannnenberg have briefly considered Feuerbach's critique of religion and so deserve our attention. We'll see from this analysis that none of them goes into the kind of detail about the broader social and ecclesiastical implications of Feuerbach's critique that I have in this book. In other words, the broader implications of Feuerbach's critique for social and ecclesiastical health are still not on the radar screen, not the way they were for Barth himself. That's another reason why

19. Henry, *God, Revelation, and Authority*, vol. 2, 66; vol. 3, 216; vol. 5, 226–27, 376; vol. 6, 31, 71, 400; Pala, *God Is Relevant*, ch. 10; Vanhoozer, *Remythologizing Theology*, 18–21, 157–61, 388–90; Vanhoozer and Trevor, *Theology and the Mirror of Scripture*; Copan, "Is God Just a Psychological Crutch for the Weak?"

the churches are in such a funk. We'll also see from this survey that, in general, these theologians don't even have theological positions that can refute Feuerbach's contention that we are reducing theology to anthropology and human experience. If you're just interested in solutions to the problems sketched in this book and don't need all the details on other theologians' failed efforts, just skip to the next chapter. The rest of this chapter is for skeptics not convinced there's anything new in this book and who think all the problems have been solved.

Paul Ricoeur and David Tracy were both famed theologians of the last century noted for their efforts to relate the Word of God to social conditions and human experience in a way that engages both in critical dialogue, and so were presumably vulnerable to Feuerbach's critique of reducing Christian claims to expressions of human experience. Ricoeur at one point referred to Feuerbach's critique of Hegel, but never measured his own hermeneutic in relation to Feuerbach. And Tracy urges that we consider Feuerbach's critique, though in such a way that we avoid reductionism, and he argues that the bigger problem for religion to address is multidisciplinary knowledge (pluralism) rather than Feuerbach's humanism.[20] Note the diminution of the importance of Feuerbach's critique. Also significant is that, as we noted previously, Ricoeur dialogued with Feuerbach, protesting this identification with Feuerbach on grounds that he does not have consciousness posit itself, for in his view the narrative influences us.[21] But Ricoeur does not address the charge that his theological statements are themselves rooted in the narrative character of history and *our experience* of it so that ultimately his approach does fall prey to Feuerbach's critique. Likewise, Tracy understands Christian language as rooted in an ontology characterized by story.[22]

When you take that position, that the Word of God is effectively rooted in human experience, you cannot withstand

20. Ricoeur, *Time and Narrative*, vol. 3, 202, 203; Tracy, *Plurality and Ambiguity*, 83, 99–100.

21. See p.45, n.32; p, 46, n.33.

22. David Tracy, *Blessed Rage for Order*, 111, 207ff.

Feuerbach's critique. Keep that in mind the next time you consider denominational or homiletical material that speaks of meaning as the fusion of God's story and our stories. Your preaching and teaching will get heard in society and among the Nones, saturated as they are by the Feuerbachian reduction of religion and everything else to human standards of measure, as just your myth, your way of coping, the reinterpreting of your story in a way that's good for you. And people in Western society today (especially Americans) are not going to accept having you try to put "your stuff" on them. No, that sort of theological appraoch won't win many friends for Christ among Nones, Xers, and Millennials.

Famed German theologians Jürgen Moltmann and Wolfhart Pannenberg run into similar problems in their dialogue with Feuerbach. Moltmann cites Feuerbach's argument that Christian faith loses when it makes its theological home in subjectivity. There is a problem if we try to restore Christianity by means of philosophy or claim that God can only be known from history or from human existence. Rather the world must be taken up into the "not yet" of hope.[23] Pannenberg finds Feuerbach to be a problem for theologies that focus only on the benefits of Christ or if, like him, theologians disassociate human nature from its origin instead of understanding humanity in terms of a reciprocal I-Thou relationship. He also proceeds to cite Barth's Christology and anthropology favorably.[24]

These points seem valid and promising strategies for others to employ in formulating theological positions in dialogue with Feuerbach, developing positions that do not fall prey to his critique. The conspiracy of silence about Feuerbach seems here broken! But ultimately Moltmann and Pannenberg have not succeeded. The problem lies with their shared theological method and view of history. They root theology in history, but it is a history interpreted in light of the future, so that Christian affirmations always have horizons. Moltmann notes that their meaning is not fixed but is always open to the future. American theologian Peter

23. Moltmann, *Theology of Hope*, 168, 170–71, 172.
24. Pannnenberg, *Jesus—God and Man*, 47, 341.

Hodgson makes a similar move.[25] You don't have a Word of God with meaning that stands over against our experience of it! For all their thoughtful observations, the positions of Moltmann and Pannenberg as well as Hodgson do not avoid the Feuerbachian critique. In view of the great influence of these theologians as well as Tracy, Ricoeur, Rahner, Lonergan, and Farley, we are reminded again of how much theology done in mainline Protestantism and Catholicism in the States as well as in Europe is vulnerable to Feuerbach's critique, and so likely to be heard as nothing more than human teachings, as somebody else's values that may or may not warrant attention.

Feminist Serene Jones sought to reject the use of Feuerbach, lest divine transcendence be lost. Francis Schüssler Fiorenza tried to provide another way around Feuerbach in the late 1970s. Drawing on a dialogue that nineteenth-century liberal German theologian Albrecht Ritschl had with Feuerbach, he contended that objective language is not desirable in theology. He spoke of having an *interest* in a religious belief without impugning objectivity.[26]

Is that really true? Interests can distort objectivity, even manufacture realities that do not exist. Interests can lead lovers to see qualities like beauty and character in each other when in fact one or both of them are not beautiful and pretty darn dishonest most of the time. Some claims that lovers make about each other are nothing more than expressions of their desires. The interests of scientists (in, for example, verifying their theories) have been known to lead to prevarication of facts in a few cases. Thus there is nothing in Fiorenza's scheme that can critique the contention that Christian claims are nothing more than expressions of the interests of believers. Jones has similar problems in her critique

25. Moltmann, *Theology of Hope*, 180–82, 187–91; Pannenberg, *Jesus—God and Man*, 97–98, 107–8; Hodgson, *God in History*, esp. 238.

26. Schüssler Fiorenza, "Responses of Barth and Ritschl to Feuerbach," 160–66; S. Jones, "This God Which Is Not One," 138. Another attempt to find a middle-ground position between liberal theology and postliberalism has been offered by Knight, *Liberalism versus Postliberalism*, esp. 268–69, 285ff. But he also never demonstrates how his proposal is immune to Feuerbach's critique.

of Feuerbach, failing to provide conceptuality to avoid reducing Christianity to mere subjectivism. Given their influence, they may embody the attempted middle-ground position between Postliberal Theology and the Chicago School of theological liberalism that Gary Dorrien characterized as the dominant position among many American theologians.

In much the same spirit, the father of Black Theology James Cone more or less addressed Feuerbach on several occasions. In one case, he merely responds to Feuerbach by referring to the Black experience, how believing in Jesus helped the community cope.[27] In this instance is he falling prey to Feuerbach's claim that religion is just wish fulfillment? Or could he be arguing more like Barth did in a book he wrote about St. Anselm that truth can only be assessed by those who immerse themselves in the existence of the Black Christian community, for only with those tools can one make a judgment about the reasonableness of Black church faithclaims? I'll be using arguments a bit like this in my own proposal in the next chapter. At other points, Cone also insists that the Word transcends all of our subjective musings, that the objective Jesus stands in judgment over all statements about truth.[28] It is not clear if Cone has successfully executed these good intentions given his other methodological commitments, correlating the Word of God with Black experience. At one point in his career he even explained his method of correlating the Word and Black experience in language used by David Tracy and Paul Ricoeur.[29] As we've noted, when you do that you reduce all theological statements to assertions that cannot stand on their own, to statements that are rooted

27. Cone, *God of the Oppressed*, 113–14; cf. Barth, *Anselm: Fides Quaerens Intellectum.*

28. Cone, *God of the Oppressed*, 1st ed., 33, 77, 109–10; Cone, "The White Church and Black Power," 82–83. For a similar analysis of these often overlooked themes in Cone, see Ware, *Methodologies of Black Theology*, 46–47, 41.

29. Cone, *God of the Oppressed*, rev. ed., 16–17 (also see 30–31, 34); Cone, *Black Theology of Liberation*, 19, 21. For a more detailed discussion of Cone's method, see my "The Legacy of James Cone: How Do We Teach It For the 21st Century?"

in human experience. Is this the outcome of Cone's thoughtful refutations, just expressions of human experience?

As we'll see in the next chapter, the answer to this question may not matter as much given the way in which the Black church seems insulated somewhat from the social trends we've been noting. Its strong storytelling traditions and biblical literacy, not just its ethnic cohesiveness, may teach the mainline some lessons about overcoming Feuerbach and our present social challenges.

One has to look long and hard for other mainline theologians dialoguing with Feuerbach since the 1960s. We have already noted Radical Orthodoxy, a movement aiming to take seriously the insights of orthodox theologians of the past even in our postmodern context. One of its proponents, Frederick Bauerschmidt, has sided with Barth in his evaluation of Feuerbach, claiming that Feuerbach is correct about Christianity when theology merely describes its subjects in terms of human self-consciousness.[30] But this point is not featured by him and his colleagues like I am trying to do in order to turn around mainline Christianity to address our latest trends.

In much the same spirit we can find a number of articles providing historical analysis of Barth's critique of Feuerbach or just Feuerbach's own thought. Barth is actually criticized in the analyses offered by Joseph C. Weber for relying on a fideism, and we have already noted how Francis Schüssler Fiorenza critiques him insofar as he offers a way around Barth's critique as well as Matthew Rose's critique of him for other reasons. Van Harvey in one book praises Feuerbach for compelling us to define our own positions, and with that point I agree. Several of these analyses (Alister McGrath, Richard Cumming, Brian Gerrish, and Manfred Vogel) share my endorsement of Barth's responses and his use of Feuerbach to critique prevailing social or theological trends of the day.[31] But none of them deal with today's marked growth of

---

30. Bauerschmidt, "Aesthetics," 206.

31. Weber, "Feuerbach, Barth, and Theological Methodology," 32; Fiorenza, "Responses of Barth and Ritschl to Feuerbach," 144–66; Rose, "Karl Barth's Failure"; Harvey, *Feuerbach's Interpretation of Religion*; for those offering a

the Nones, nor even make clear (with the possible exception of McGrath) that failure to heed Feuerbach's critique is contributing to secularism. Feuerbach's critique and its implications for contemporary theology is certainly not a hot topic in the academy, and so it is not surprising that the church has not made much of an impact on current social trends and continues losing ground.

It is interesting to note that even among those whom we would expect a dialogue with Feuerbach and a recognition of how the failure to heed his critique of Christianity is undermining our religious and social life there is not a lot of effective response. The fathers of Postliberalism and Biblical Narrative Theology, George Lindbeck and Hans Frei, did not typically dialogue with Feuerbach or address his critique of religion. Lindbeck nowhere refers to Feuerbach, and Frei simply noted that for Barth, Feuerbach "constitutes the bad conscience of modern theology," that "true theology begins precisely where the problems discovered by Feuerbach and Strauss are seen."[32] Why Frei did not further elaborate on these problems is one of the reasons we need this book.

---

historical analysis, see Lindberg, "Luther and Feuerbach"; Glasse, "Barth on Feuerbach"; Hodgson, *God in History*, 50, 138; Hans Schwarz, "Eschatology," in Braaten and Jenson, *Christian Dogmatics*, 2:475; Carl Braaten, "The Person of Jesus Christ," in Braaten and Jenson, *Christian Dogmatics*, 1:540; Carl Braaten, "Prolegomena to Christian Dogmatics," in Braaten and Jenson, *Christian Dogmatics*, vol. 1:24. The fact that this widely used Lutheran textbook does not grapple with Feuerbach's critique but merely reports his views is another indication of how that critique has been effectively muzzled in mainline denominations. Braaten's more recent laments about the structure of the Evangelical Lutheran Church in America as a source of its woes misses the main point regarding why the theological position he and his generation articulated resulted in the Protestant liberalism and theologies unable to critique present social trends that dominate today.

Those supporting Barth's critique include Cumming, "Revelation as Apologetic Category"; Vogel, "The Barth-Feuerbach Confrontation"; Gerrish, "Feuerbach's Religious Illusion"; McGrath, *Bridge-Building*; McGrath, *A Scientific Theology*; McGill, "An Interview with Alister McGrath," *DTS Magazine*, December 1, 2012, https://voice.dts.edu/article/an-interviewwith-alister-mcgraith-mcgill-junny/.

32. Frei, *Types of Christian Theology*, 11. Frei also delivered a talk on Feuerbach at the 1965 annual meeting of the American Academy of Religion, but this does not seem to have been particularly central to his work.

Eminent theologian Stanley Hauerwas is often associated with the postliberalism of his teachers. True enough, he did dialogue with Feuerbach on several occasions, as he sees the controversial philosopher's critique as a caution against theology translating into "secularism" (another way of warning against mixing the Word with human experience) or cites Barth as warning us that "worldliness" in theology falls prey to Feuerbach's critique.[33] But as effective as these points are, in line with the issues I have been raising, Hauerwas's own constructive work may fall short. Besides critiques raised against him as a fideist (which I think are unfounded), he has not succeeded as much as he thinks in presenting a version of Christianity that is truly a distinct society that is unique in comparison with the latest social fads. For at least sometimes he seems, like Ricoeur and Tracy, to understand the Christian narrative in light of the narrative character of selfhood, to interpret Christian claims in light of human experience.[34] In that case even Hauerwas has failed clearly to provide a version of the faith free from the specter of being just another human option. If America's best (*Time Magazine* named him America's best theologian) fails on that score, is it any wonder that the public still suspects Christianity may be nothing too special, just another not very interesting option?

What's become of Feuerbach? He may not be getting much attention in academic theology and so not in the seminary classroom, in denominational headquarters, or in the pulpit. But he's still around, haunting a lot of modern theology.

33. Hauerwas, "Reforming Theological Ethics," 52; Hauerwas, *With the Grain of the Universe*, 35–36.

34. Hauerwas, *A Community of Character*, 144; Hauerwas et al., *Truthfulness and Tragedy*, 21, 35, 38. In fairness he seems to qualify this tendency to interpret the Christian story in light of some universal story in his *Community of Character*, 96–97, 149–50.

WHY IT MATTERS

The critiques I have been offering above of allies (and anyone who wants to avoid a theology vulnerable to the reduction of God's Word to human experience is an ally) are not the main point of this chapter or the book. It will take the formation of a significant coalition of those committed to the transcendent, authoritative Word of God to get the church in the West out of its funk, to stem the growth of the Nones. The main point of this book is not whether my critiques of these colleagues are founded; nor is the book's main point about my own proposal in the next chapter in articulating a theological perspective to overcome Feuerbach's critique and to change pop-culture perceptions of Christianity. The critique of prevailing theological and denominational trends is *the* issue. So let's review one more time why not wrestling with Feuerbach's critique of Christianity matters.

Ludwig Feuerbach's critique of Christianity—the belief that Christian teachings are just ways of human beings expressing their yearnings—is soundly ensconced in pop culture and the thought of the Nones. To the degree the prevailing theologies of our day are vulnerable to that critique (and they are vulnerable), Christian ideas will be received with little interest in American and European society, as nothing more than another option for self-fulfillment, and not a very interesting one at that. The more the churches reflect the concern for relevance, the more likely they will reinforce these trends. By neglecting Feuerbach's critique, acting as if we've never heard of it or as if it is not relevant to our situation, it is easier for the theological and denominational establishments to perpetuate their present modes of operation, leading them to become more and more ensconced in such thinking and ways of being as they seek to become more and more saturated with the latest trends. The best way forward: to find ways of doing theology like Karl Barth advocated, to present a version of Christianity that is clearly not an option like the available ones, the Word of God that is not in any way perceived as dependent on us but in all its majesty and authority confronts all our present visions and changes them, almost like a scientific theory or love does.

What will critics of this book do with the preceding point? One angle may be to critique the shortcomings of my constructive proposal in the next chapter. But since that is not my primary concern in this book, if anyone can do better work on that and still avoid Feuerbach's critique, I am happy to defer to them. My fear is that such a critique will take the focus off Feuerbach's critique. Another angle may be to criticize my analysis of the theologians in this chapter, to critique my treatment of Feuerbach or of Barth's critique. That will not bother me too much either, unless such critiques allow church leaders and theologians to dodge Feuerbach's critique of their own theological positions and leadership styles. And then of course there is always the possibility of no reviews or engagements with the book at all. As we've seen, this has largely been the establishment's style in dealing with Feuerbach's critique since the nineteenth century.

When you can't refute an argument, dodge it. When an argument threatens your position, it is easier to ignore its points. If this appeal to Feuerbach's insights—to the vulnerability of the dominant models of theology as a way of explaining why the churches are in such a funk—is off base, there is no reason why the theological establishment should not greet this work with resounding critique. But if that does not happen, readers, if all the criticisms of this book dodge this main point or it gets completely ignored, then maybe, just maybe, it's because the establishment and national office staffs can't get around Feuerbach's critique of their own positions and ways of functioning. That's why we need to get church leaders to start hearing about Feuerbach.

5

How Barth Could Still Help

It's Not Too Late, but It Will Take
Some Common-Sense Tweaking

Despite the problems critics have noted with Barth's approach and the increasing neglect of his theology, we've already established the penetrating character of his critique of prevailing trends in contemporary theology. The question is how we can still be informed by his insights in trying to find a theological perspective that can help the church get out of its funk.

In fact, there are overlooked aspects of Barth's thought that can be of great assistance, especially his views on how to interpret Scripture. Let's start there. In making many of my points I will be influenced by my own appropriations of Postliberal Theology we've noted in previous chapters. But this is not a chapter about the views of the earliest framers of this and a related Canonical approach, George Lindbeck and Hans Frei or Brevard Childs. I am moving beyond their proposals, even correcting shortcomings I see in their thinking, in order to find ways in which we can get the mainline churches out of their funk, to present models of Christian thought that really can get the Nones' attention. I believe that we can take Barth's insights in ways these scholars missed, utilizing common-sense traditions of American culture as well as American pragmatism, gaining insights from traditions that are not being so hurt by membership erosion (the Black church, immigrant churches, and even evangelicals), and exploiting American veneration of science as a way of escaping the relativism that traps us in the West. But remember: even if you don't like these moves, and can do better, don't forget the previous chapters and how we've seen that the theological establishment has essentially conceded Feuerbach's critique, and that that's why the mainline denominations' version of the Christian faith is no longer seen in pop culture as a genuine, even intriguing alternative to everyday American life.

The first step to remedy these dynamics that I propose is to get the Bible away from being confused with a history book or a science book. It is not making these sorts of claims. Instead it is a great set of stories and ideas that change lives. This approach sets the Bible free for a hearing without having to defend that the miracles happened or the Genesis version of creation in relation to what we know about the big bang or evolution. It sets us free from the concept of the Bible as salvation-history used by Karl Barth and other Neo-Orthodox theologians, a claim which, as we observed in the previous chapter, seems to rely on an intellectually dishonest ambiguity.

The approach that I am advocating does not deny that the events reported in the Bible may have happened or that the accounts are not true. More on that later, but those questions logically emerge after we consider the biblical accounts and become conversant with them. At the outset, we can remind people that theology is a science and that our claims as Christians are testable, but first let's observe the data.

BIBLICAL DATA AND HOW TO CONSIDER IT

Scientists have to make decisions about what they are studying and what means to use in studying that data. Certain formal agreements or paradigms guide research and study of data.[1] Theologians also have some formal agreements or paradigms to guide their research. All of them agree that the Bible and its stories are a starting point, a (if not *the*) source for data. What is in the Bible? We've already ruled out it being primarily history or scientific data (though there might be some points of contact with these disciplines). Many would agree with postliberal theologians who have claimed that the Bible is primarily a book of stories (narratives), especially centered on God's Work through Jesus or describing the identify of Jesus Christ. And those parts of the Bible that are not narratives (like the epistles, psalms, prophecies) are best understood as commentaries on the narratives.[2] These are the data for doing theology, and these data are what we present to the church and the general public.

Narratives, notably the biblical narratives, absorb us into their world. When you read a good realistic novel or a historical narrative you begin to feel like you know the characters or are part of the story. A quotation by prominent literary critic Erich Auerbach, who has influenced Postliberal Theology, is relevant:

> The Bible's claim to truth is not only . . . urgent . . . it is tyrannical—it excludes other claims. The world of the Scripture stories is not satisfied with claiming to be a historically true reality—it insists that it is the only real world, is destined for autocracy. All other scenes, issues, and ordinances have no right to appear independently of it, and it is promised that all of them, the history of mankind, will be given their due place within its frame, will be subordinated to it. . . . Far from seeking, like Homer, merely to make us forget our reality for a few hours, it seeks to overcome our reality: we are to fit our own life

1. Scientists and historians of science characterizing the scientific method this way include Kuhn, *The Structure of Scientific Revolutions*, 9–10, 36ff., 145; Hawking and Mlodinow, *The Grand Design*, 46, 172.

2. See Frei, "Theological Reflections on the Accounts of Jesus' Death and Resurrection," 43; Lindbeck, "The Church's Mission to a Postmodern Culture," 41. For much of what follows, see my *A Common Sense Theology*, esp. 19–54, 153ff.

into its world, to feel ourselves to be elements in its structure of universal history.[3]

As we have observed, there was a time in America and Western Europe, like most premodern cultures, when Christian stories and images dominated public discourse and were the basis for interpreting what was transpiring socially and individually. We have seen how this has changed as a result of secularism. Now the primary images are individualism, self-fulfillment, self-sufficiency, openness, flexibility, and material prosperity, mixed with a certain deference to scientific findings and a yearning for non-binding communities (when they fit our needs). I've been arguing that as long as the churches continue to translate the Word into categories like these, the church loses, because Christians are then providing nothing more than what people can already get from the world.

The agenda that I and like-minded colleagues propose is to get the strange stories of the Bible into society (strange in comparison to the Western myths most Americans and Western Europeans, especially younger generations, are living with and using to interpret their lives). It's gotten harder and harder to do so as biblical literacy among Christians declines.[4] This is no doubt related to the de-emphasis on learning the literal Word of God in most mainline denominational educational literature. But if mainline Christians could begin to get Bible stories out in broader society about Jesus' and the disciples' engagement with the poor (Matt 19:21; Acts 4:32—5:11), about how Jesus gives life in the midst of death (John 11:25–26), stories about truly inclusive communities that last through thick and thin (Gen 17; Eph 1:22–23), about finding life through self-denial (Rom 6:1–14; Col 3:1–7), about how God does not favor the wealthy (Matt 19:24; Mark 4:19), and about God's presence with his creation in everyday life (Eph 1:9–10),

---

3. Auerbach, *Mimesis*, 14–15; cf. Frei, *The Eclipse of Biblical Narrative*, 3; Lindbeck, "The Church's Mission to a Postmodern Culture," 38; Childs, *Introduction to the Old Testament as Scripture*, 143.

4. Lindbeck, "The Church's Mission to a Postmodern Culture," 38, 44ff. For more hard data on growing biblical illiteracy, see Barna Research, "51% of Churchgoers Don't Know of the Great Commission."

reminders that work is not done to please the boss or just to make
a few bucks but to please God (Col 3:23–24), about how we flawed,
pretty darn selfish human beings are yet affirmed and made to do
good things by God (Rom 7:14–23; Eph 2:4–10), and about eternal
life so that death does not have the final say (Mark 16; 1 Cor 15),
we might be presenting unique options to Western society and the
Nones—options they are not hearing much about.

Insofar as in narratives we identify with characters who are in
relation to God, and in the biblical narrative the characters are in
relation to God, another impact of becoming immersed in the biblical narrative is that we are more likely to experience the sacred.
And then in turn we might more readily experience the sacred in
all aspects of our lives as we interpret daily life in light of the biblical accounts and themes. Thus construing the Bible as narrative in
which we are the characters seems a credible way of responding
to secularism, for in embodying Peter, Paul, Moses, etc., we are in
touch with God in our daily lives.

In order to communicate these countercultural, appealing
themes to the masses, Christians are going to have to be able to express these themes spontaneously, to be skilled at looking at daily
life in light of these insights. That means not just learning how to
communicate these themes attractively in the media, though that
will help our Christian education tasks. We're going to have to de-
vote years to Christian re-education in parishes, in Sunday schools
and Bible studies. We are going to have to break out of the molds
of most mainline denominational educational strategies, cut down
on the arts and crafts, the playacting and the singing that take up
the majority of the education time allotted. We are actually going
to have to start teaching the Bible and its stories again. "Oh, but
that won't interest our members, won't be relevant and interesting
to them," critics in many pulpits and denominational offices will
say. But dominant techniques aren't working (for all the reasons
I've been citing).

Teaching Bible stories as the engaging stories that they are,
luring us into them so that we identify with them, making clear
that they are the hard data for guiding research and living, not just

the opinions of a bunch of ancient Jews, can answer a lot of skepticism. Let's get clear on the sort of theological presuppositions we'll need to make these things happen, to turn the churches around.

TOWARD A COMMONSENSE SCIENTIFIC THEOLOGICAL METHOD THAT WORKS

Just interpreting the Bible as an overall narrative does not free us from Feuerbach's critique. We have already observed cases in which Feuerbach's critique pertains if the biblical narrative is construed as an instance of a broader philosophical belief about the narrative character of human nature (Ricoeur and Tracy). To avoid that, we need a mode of interpreting Scripture, a model for doing theology that allows for descriptive meaning, literal meaning and truth of God's Word, that cannot be discredited by Feuerbach's critique of Christianity and so be heard as just the opinion of a bunch of folks who call themselves Christian. And as American society illustrates today, immersed as it is in relativism, subjectivism, and the Kantian turn to the subject so that everything people say or teach is just their version of truth, what works for them, where truth is the latest fad on the internet or what gets the most likes, when opinions are presented they are not debated. You either say or post nothing (because you don't want to offend anybody) or you demonize the other. Christian teaching will not get a hearing or exert much public impact unless its authority is publicly plausible. It won't get much attention if just presented as someone's version of truth.

This is not just a matter of mainline Christianity adopting a different way of reading the Bible. It is a way of making clear to the broader public that the Bible really says what the church says it means, is offering a real alternative to our subjectivity. The ancient text has more authority, is better able to capture society's attention than some contemporary Christian's version of it. Consequently for the church to be able to proclaim to the public that it offers the Bible's Word, not just what some Christians think, makes a real dialogue with the biblical text possible. Now the door is open for critics, not inhibited by the "everyone's entitled to their own opinion so just ignore" syndrome, to say "yes" or "no" to the authority of the biblical witness.

The Word of God understood in this way is tyrannical, as the New Critics remind us. These stories, like a lot of good books, have their way with us. And for Millennials, often caught up in their subjectivity and malaise, getting caught up in stories or images bigger than they are, is something for which they have been searching. For as we've already noted, the Millennials and other younger generations are not happy, though they are always searching for meaning in life and work, according to a 2016 Gallup poll report.

The continuing influence of the Religious Right and the African-American church, segments of Christianity not so caught up in the subjectivist relativism (the idea that our experience or cultural context or gender conditions what we say) like the mainline churches have, illustrates why, like these traditions, we need models of interpretation and theology that get ourselves out of the way, that can truly claim that we speak God's and the historic church's Word.

There is a larger audience ready to listen to the idea of a descriptive, literal meaning and to authoritative claims, even an openness to scientific findings that override mere subjectivism, than the cultural gurus might lead us to believe. True enough, as we have noted, belief in descriptive meaning and descriptive truth has taken a hit in American society. But the belief that truth can be achieved (at least by scientists) was still in place according to a 2014 poll of *The Economist*. And a majority believes that morality is not just a private matter according to a 2016 Barna Research poll.[5] As we'll see, this is in line with old American beliefs in common sense.

But what sense does it make in our individualistic, relativistic, therapeutically defined context to refer to a text's literal sense or descriptive meaning? What about relevance in our programming,

5. *Economist*/YouGov, "Many Americans Are Scientific Skeptics"; Barna Research, "The End of Absolutes: America's New Moral Code."

teaching, and preaching? We need to target our market, the skeptics would say. On this point, Karl Barth provides a little-noticed model for interpretation that deserves a lot more attention and has been overlooked by a number of my readers of past books.

According to Barth, it seems, one need not choose between descriptive literal meaning and a reading of Scripture that takes human experience and cultural context into account. He does this by distinguishing three distinct elements of biblical interpretation: (1) *explicatio*, (2) *meditatio*, and (3) *applicatio*. The first phase is very modest in its aims; it is nothing more than an effort to explain the biblical Word, to obtain an "accurate picture" of what is "intrinsically intelligible." Granted in subsequent phases, especially at the point of application, one's context or faith commitments play an indisputable role. But in the initial phase of *explication* we must "leave to this object . . . the freedom to assert and affirm over against these presuppositions of ours, and in certain cases compel us to adopt new presuppositions."[6]

When the distinction of these phases and the very modest aims of the first phase are kept in mind, the idea that descriptive meaning of certain texts is possible may become more palatable for modern theologians and society in general. (Of course, it is only narrative texts or epistles that are capable of being understood in terms of a literal, descriptive meaning. Only these literary genres "mean what they say," as Frei once put it.[7] You typically read

---

6. Barth, *Church Dogmatics*, I/2:722–40; cf. Frei, *Types of Christian Theology*, 92–94. Of course, Barth himself may not endorse the idea that at some stage in the process the identification of a text's (or concept's) normative meaning is possible. But in *Church Dogmatics*, I/2:736, he does claim that the proof of openness to the Word of God, presumably in all the phases of interpretation, is that it leads to assimilation (the experience of the Word of God).

7. Frei, "Response to 'Narrative Theology: An Evangelical Appraisal,'" 22. For affirmations of the possibility of normative interpretation by postliberal theologians and their allies, see Frei, "Remarks in Connection with a Theological Proposal"; Frei, *The Identity of Jesus Christ*, xv, xvii; Lindbeck, *The Nature of Doctrine*, 116, 101–2, 68; Childs, *Introduction to the Old Testament as Scripture*, 77, 72–74; Childs, *The New Testament as Canon*, 24, 38–39, 292, 546. The importance of distinguishing the kind of biblical literature with which we are dealing in order to determine what sorts of claims a text is making is

any narrative or letter in this way. But no claim is made regarding the possibility of identifying normative meaning of the Psalms or apocalyptic and prophetic literature. You don't try to interpret dreams or poetry literally.) This (Barthian) scheme makes place for personal experience and a sensitivity to social context (including sociological and even psychological categories) in theology in the later stages of the process of interpretation, when we meditate on a text's or concept's existential meaning or go about appropriating its commitments. Only at the logically, if not temporally, prior phase is the identification of the descriptive, objective meaning of Christian concepts deemed a possibility.

Making sure that there is experiential and social impact on the interpretation of a text at later phases of interpretation is just common sense. No two sermons and no two mediations on the same texts/concepts are identical, nor should they be. But all should be able to agree that Mark 16 is a report of the resurrection and the disciples' amazement about it. Believing in the descriptive meaning of texts/concepts when all interpreters agree that the language game is interpreting narrative texts makes common sense in daily life outside of the theological guild and when not talking multiculturalism with church leaders. Likewise, in the language-game of driving in the US, when we see a red sign with the letters S-T-O-P while driving, my African-American colleagues, my Hispanic son-in-law, the gay bishop of my region, and women who know English from across the globe know that they should stop their cars. Different backgrounds and experiences do not change the text's meaning in this case. But whether we are happy to stop or glad for the break, whether we in fact stop or run the stoplight, whether we look with suspicion about cops who might stop us, are functions of our personal situation and mindset, of the interpretive tools and suppositions we bring to encounter with this data.

Likewise, the theory of atoms is the same for scientists and non-scientists, for educated people of all ethnicities all over the globe. But reactions will differ on whether the use of this

---

advocated by the leader of the Human Genome Project, Francis Collins, and Karl Giberson, in *The Language of Science and Faith*, 94.

information for purposes of military defense or as a source of energy is welcomed. Again, our differences will be functions of our politics, economic situations in life (the CEO of a major gasoline producer will be different from one who has investments in nuclear energy), and where we live. It is obvious that the model adopted by Barth and some of his theological heirs is a promising resource for taking seriously the intentions of theologians and church leaders concerned with the relevance of faith while also possibly avoiding the Feuerbachian critique (because with this model you can indigenize your theology and still affirm that an objective Word of God unites the various ways of appropriating it, and so the customized utterances of faith are rooted in an objective authority).

Before proceeding to the issue of how affirming this objective Word of God makes sense intellectually and will communicate in our postmodern context, I need to emphasize this last point for critics. In previous books in which I articulated Barth's model of the three distinct elements of biblical interpretation, several critics did not read what I wrote very carefully. It was alleged by these theologians/homileticians that I had missed how it is sometimes necessary to employ concepts drawn from other disciplines or that I had misinterpreted Hans Frei regarding his use of such disciplines like sociology, focusing only on his use of the literary analytic school of New Criticism.[8] My embrace of this model from Barth and attribution of it to Frei obviously puts these critiques to rest as I conceded in my previous books and again here that theology can use a number of intellectual tools (not just literary criticism) in an ad hoc way.

These critics also overstate Frei's apparent turn away from reliance on New Criticism to explicate the literal meaning of biblical texts. He never intended to use New Criticism as a general theory into which the biblical narrative is subsumed. And he always made clear (as I did in one of my books) that if you use New Criticism

8. For books in which I invoked Barth's model of the different elements or moves in biblical interpretation, see my *Integrity of Biblical Narrative*, 35; *A Common Sense Theology*, 37–38. For the critics, see Pembroke, *Divine Therapeia and the Sermon*, esp. 58; Campbell, *Preaching Jesus*, 181ff.; Brothers, *Distance in Preaching*, 114–15.

it is only in the sense that this literary analytic is a disguised Christian understanding. The literal sense of the biblical narrative governs and bends whatever general categories it shares. But with that qualification he insisted that a literal reading of Scripture was appropriate under the auspices of New Criticism.[9]

It should be evident now as we aim for more specifics about how to overcome Feuerbach's critique by clearly establishing that it is possible to identify a biblical text's or theological statement's literal meaning, not conditioned by human experience. We need to turn to an ad hoc use of the New Critical School of literary analysis, but will see that use of such a tool along with anthropology, pragmatism, neurobiology, and American common sense can also help us find intellectually attractive ways of talking about Christianity's truth.

We've already established that the Bible cannot be considered a science or history book. This is where literary analysis becomes relevant as a tool for interpretation of the Christian book. The school of New Criticism, coupled with insights of twentieth-century Austrian philosopher Ludwig Wittgenstein, anthropologist Clifford Geertz, as well as an appreciation of how the scientific method functions can help us make these intentions concrete. Let's begin with New Criticism.

The literary analytic school termed "New Criticism" originated early in the twentieth century, in a period when aesthetic theory was dominated by a breed of Romanticism and a "scientism" that threatened to devalue all art as a valid mode of knowledge, so that only science or history was deemed competent to determine truth. Not unlike today, nineteenth-century literary and biblical studies were dominated by the use of historical-critical tools to such an extent that the meaning of texts was reduced to the status of mere "expressions" of its immediate historical and cultural contexts, of which the texts' authors were only representative. Literary analysts like I. A. Richards in England and Ramon Jakobson in Russia reacted against these dynamics, insisting that the meaning of texts is

9. Frei, "The 'Literal Reading' of Biblical Narrative in the Christian Tradition: Does It Stretch or Will It Break?," esp. 185–86.

related to their structure, not their authors' intentions and context or to what the text refers that preoccupies science.[10] It is in the text that we find a text's meaning, not by bringing historical, psychological, or scientific concerns to bear on it.

These scholars opened the way to the development in the 1920s in America of New Criticism. Among its primary leaders, many with roots in Yale University, were William Wimsatt, Robert Penn Warren, and Cleanth Brooks. Like Richards and Jakobson, New Critics insisted that the structure of a literary text, not its historical truth or even its author's intention, is the crucial matter in interpretation. Indeed, a literary text has its own autonomy.[11]

Just as literature can only be evaluated on its own terms according to this cutting-edge literary theory, so it follows that on these grounds the Bible is not validly evaluated by criteria other than its own, not by historical, cultural, psychological, or scientific criteria. This conclusion is supported by other intellectual currents. The point is most in line with the later writings of Ludwig Wittgenstein. In his study of language, he came to see language as a function of its use in a context. In his view we may call the context for a language's use a "language-game." In it, we identify certain objects with the words and learn to respond appropriately to the words. The different languages are games. Likewise, special uses of languages (chess, football, sociology, Christianity, etc.) are language-games. Thus meaning is the use of the words in a language-game. This entails that truth is a function of the language-game in which the claim is made.[12] You can't judge a statement true of false or

10. Richards, *Practical Criticism*, 24, 203–4; Richards, *Principles of Literary Criticism*, 28–29, 264ff.; Ramon Jakobson, as quoted in Ejxenbaum, "The Theory of the Formal Method," 18; Jakobson, "The Dominant," 83–84; Jakobson, "Poetry of Grammar and a Grammar of Poetry," 603.

For a characterization of the context of the time when these movements emerged, see Wimsatt and Brooks, *Literary Criticism*, 2:533–34. For a more detailed discussion of New Criticism, see my *A Common Sense Theology*, esp. 167ff.

11. Wimsatt, *The Verbal Icon*, 3ff., 87; Brooks and Warren, *Understanding Fiction*, 25.

12. Wittgenstein, *Philosophical Investigations*, 7, 83, 136, 139.

know its meaning apart from the rules of the language game. For example, the statement "fouls are penalized" is true in the games of basketball and soccer, but not in baseball (as there is no penalty for a foul if you already have two strikes). Likewise the game of Christian theology. You can't make judgments about Christian claims or even understand them unless you take into account the rules of faith. A negative judgment about these claims on purely scientific or historic suppositions no more negates their truth than a basketball player operating on that game's suppositions can prove that a foul in baseball violates the rules. This should be acceptable to those with an avangelical theological orientation.[13] Of course, Wittgenstein will allow that some language-games overlap in "family resemblances."[14] The games of American football and rugby have a lot in common, as do all the Romance languages. At some points the words and principles of these overlapping games converge. The math you use in the game of mathematics you find useful in the games of architecture and physics.

It is interesting that the distinction between Christian claims, history, and science has sound intellectual backing. You may not want to use these insights when trying to teach the faith to postmodern Christians, the Nones, or in social gatherings. They are perhaps too abstract to get attention to the simple, startling claim Christians want to make: that just because the Bible teaches some things that can't be historically or scientifically verified, which may not seem to make sense in our individualistic, therapeutic cultural values, does not mean that its teachings are not true or meaningful. If challenged you now have some arguments about how credible that claim is. But I think Christians can make that point more concisely just by noting that our claims are in fact scientifically credible.

---

13. At least evangelicals with a Presuppositionalist Method like Carl F. H. Henry: see *God, Revelation, and Authority*, 1:215, 3:247, 428; Schaeffer, *The God Who Is There*, esp. 87ff; Christian Reformed Church, *The Nature and Extent of Biblical Authority*, 13–14, 23. This method claims that arguments for Christian truth are valid only if employed in the context of initial presuppositions that God/Christ exists and that he has infallibly revealed himself.

14. Wittgenstein, *Philosophical Investigations*, 67.

As we've noted, most Americans think that science is the one discipline left in which you can find objective truth. Part of that is a function of a false understanding of what science provides. More and more scientists are willing to concede that science does not answer all questions. Its focus is on explaining the dynamics of what is happening, but it is less equipped to examine the purpose (the why) of these phenomena. Science does not provide a full-blown worldview![15] Consequently, even scientists seem to concede that Christianity is not necessarily ruled out by scientific findings to date.

Christians need to get this word out in the public. Stories about creation in Genesis and other references to it can live together with the theory of evolution and the big bang theory. They address different issues. But this is not to say that Christian truth claims and scientific findings (or those of the historian) have no overlap. To insist that the Bible is not a book of science and history does not mean that the Bible's claims have no bearing on science. Sometimes the Bible reports what happens or refers to the natural world. No less eminent a scientist than Francis Collins, the geneticist who spearheaded the famous Human Genome Project, has made this point.[16]

We might make the point by thinking about how we might analyze a field of flowers in a garden in suburbia. We could do it aesthetically, commenting on their beauty. A biological analysis would engage us in what caused the flowers to grow. We might analyze their growth historically, noting when the seeds were purchased, when planted, and the amount of work involved in nurturing the growth. Or we might analyze the phenomena theologically, noting God's role in the process—all different analyses, each valid in their own way. And yet the analyses overlap; they do not necessarily cancel out each other.

I'll return to this point later, considering in what sense the Bible might be compatible with what is true in relation to science

15. John Polkinghorne, cited in Giberson and Collins, *Language of Science and Faith*, 107–8.

16. Giberson and Collins, *Language of Science and Faith*, 10.

and history, a point that is crucial for its credibility in our post-modern ethos. But at this point, we have established with solid academic and even scientific footing the sense in which biblical and theological claims can be said to be true on their own grounds, that it is not valid to pronounce their falsity just by arguing that these claims are not historically or scientifically verifiable.

Critics of Christianity might still object that this understanding of Christian claims as distinct from science and history does not avoid Feuerbach's critique. After all, the Bible's narratives are expressions of human creativity/experience, it could be contended. But this argument overlooks the New Critical interpretive assumptions I am employing. Recall how we noted above that the interests of this approach focus on the text to be interpreted, not the author's intentions or experience. And the biblical text or Christian teachings have their own descriptive meaning not dependent on their authors' intended meaning about which one might speculate. (This New Critical approach that rejects focusing on the author's intention as the locus of meaning flies in the face of lots of modern biblical scholarship, which may explain why such scholarship has not captured the attention of many preachers and those in the pews. This dominant model intuitively feels like a reduction of Bible teachings to human experience.) Christians are people who believe that God had a hand in writing the Bible and the various Christian doctrines, that their literal meaning is his, not necessarily reducible to the intended meaning of their human authors through whom God has worked. Of course this belief cannot be proven, but as we'll note, it can be a valid hypothesis for the faithful unless or until evidence is put forth to prove that God had no involvement in these teachings. Thus far no such evidence exists.

In order for this approach to work, we first need to clarify how to determine the meaning of biblical and theological claims, in what sense it is possible at the *explicatio* stage of interpretation to assert the descriptive meaning of Christian claims in our post-Kantian world. If we can't, then this proposal too falls prey to Feuerbach's critique.

FINDING COMMON MEANING

We've already dealt with the factors that create skepticism about a literal, descriptive meaning of texts. If we cannot keep the interpreter's experience out of the meaning, then the meaning of God and the Word would be a function of human experience.[17] The theological heirs of Barth need a view of meaning that can be determined even by those outside the universe of discourse, so that you don't have to be a Christian in order to understand the Bible like Christians do, as long as you share their interpretive suppositions.[18] Recall at this point that in claiming descriptive meaning is possible I am not ruling out input from other sources at later stages of interpretation (when we meditate on or apply biblical references).

To get to the literal sense you need to share the formal interpretive suppositions of the church (though not necessarily believe them). We have already sketched these suppositions, regarding the construal of Scripture as a realistic narrative, including texts that are commentaries on it, and that it is not a book of science or history, but one making Christian claims that functions authoritatively for the church. In order to rectify previous misinterpretations of my work noted earlier, I emphasize with Hans Frei that these interpretive suppositions employed are formal, not material.[19]

A formal rule just determines the rule of a game, such as the rule in basketball that only five players may be on the court at a time. This rule is formal, not a material rule like the directive of a run-and-gun team that always seeks to penetrate the defense and look for a fast break with every opportunity. When we all agree on these formal rules, just noted, it is possible for all readers to agree on the Bible's literal sense (in those texts where there is a literal sense, because their genre as a narrative or epistle demands a literal reading).

---

17. Frei, "Remarks in Connection with a Theological Proposal," 32.

18. See n. 7 above. Also see J. Smith, *Who's Afraid of Relativism?*, 134.

19. Frei, *Types of Christian Theology*, 41. Also see n. 7 above.

I agree with Hans Frei and the historic Christian tradition that discerning the literal sense is a communal enterprise, not just the work of the isolated scholar using the correct literary analytic method. Thus I can affirm his rules concerning the literal sense: (1) it is the consensus of the Christian community; (2) it is the enactment of the intention of the text (a point in some tension with New Criticism's critique of concern with the author's intention, but an affirmation of this literary analytic method's commitment to discussing the text and not what is "behind it"); and (3) there is no distinction between the sense of the text and its subject matter, and the subject matter is Christocentric.[20] With these commitments we see Frei's and Barth's insistence that the literal sense of Scripture still governs and bends whatever general categories it shares is heartily endorsed.[21] The latest fashions in the community cannot overturn the literal sense, which both the faithful and academic observers can discern. Meaning is not a function of the community's experience.

This approach entails that the guild of biblical scholars rethink what they are doing, that we distort the Bible when we focus on the historical background of texts or presume that the biblical authors' intentions are at odds with the way in which the church has understood them. Biblical scholarship and interpretation on these grounds need to be in touch with the hermeneutical consensus of the church. If that is not done, Old and New Testament scholarship is not exposing students to the texts' literal/Christian meanings.

This idea that the literal sense of Scripture is determined by rules of consensus in the Christian community has a lot in common with how science operates according to consensus in the guild regarding the paradigms of consensus in the community that in turn directs the research and are accepted.[22] The literal sense of

20. Frei, *Types of Christian Theology*, 15–16; Frei, "Theology and Interpretation of Narrative," 112.

21. Frei, "'Literal Reading' of Biblical Narrative," 67.

22. This description of how science operates has been offered by Kuhn, *Structure of Scientific Revolutions*, 4, 9–10, 36ff., 145. The applicability of this

Scripture, authentic tradition that any student of Christianity can identify, directs the research.

Surprisingly (to many academics and proponents of the media worldview) the position that I and many postliberal theologians advocate has a number of defenders that give this commitment academic and social credibility. We have already noted how in everyday life descriptive meaning seems possible, as when we observe a stop sign or the final score of a basketball game. Of course, our appropriations and feelings about these facts will differ. Likewise, observations illustrating the law of gravity are not altered by the ethnicity or gender of the scientist. But a number of other intellectual tools, most of which we have already noted as resources for developing a theological perspective that does not fall prey to Feuerbach's critique, allow for the possibility of identifying the descriptive meaning of texts or data. Let's begin with Anglo-American New Criticism.

We have already noted how New Criticism can be of service to the post-Barthian theology we've been developing, with its insistence on interpreting texts on grounds of what they actually say (their canonical structure), not in terms of their historical genesis. New Critics also help in the critique of Feuerbach by positing the possibility of a text's "public knowledge." One New Critic, William Wimsatt, has written,

> We argued that the design or intention of the author is neither available nor desirable as a standard for judging the success of a work of literary art. . . . The poem is not the critic's own and not the author's (it is detached from the author at birth and goes about the world beyond his power to intend about it or control it). The poem belongs to the public. It is embodied in language, the peculiar possession of the public, and it is about the human being, an object of public knowledge.[23]

---

description for how theology should operate has been noted by Lindbeck, "The Church's Mission to a Postmodern Culture," 50–51.

23. Wimsatt, *Verbal Icon*, 3, 5.

The idea of "public knowledge" entails descriptive meaning. Public knowledge is something we all have; we all start on the same page and can converse about it. It presupposes objective, descriptive meaning.

This concept of a common, public knowledge also has roots in the American system and the society it has nurtured. Indeed, American society was shaped by the Scottish Enlightenment, which was grounded in Empiricism, and predisposed to accept the possibility that people can reason together. A crucial, often overlooked intellectual debt of America's founders was to the philosophy of Scottish Common Sense Realism. Thomas Jefferson reflects his appreciation of this philosophy on a number of occasions, and the only clergyman to sign the Declaration of Independence, the primary professor of James Madison at Princeton, John Witherspoon, was an advocate of Common Sense Realism.[24] Consider the "self-evident truths" of the Declaration of Independence and also the concept of "consent of the governed" in the Constitution's preamble. Both of these commitments stem from Common Sense Realism.[25]

Another commitment of this philosophical school crucial for our purposes is its commitment to Common Sense readings of texts, that we can establish the descriptive meaning of a text. The primary spokesman of the Scottish philosophy, Thomas Reid, speaks of a "common meaning" of words, learned from our common community experience, and about which all can agree.[26] Once again we observe an intellectual precedent for challenging today's mad celebration of pluralism and relativism.

24. Jefferson, "Letter to Dugald Stewart," 1488; Jefferson, "Letter to Robert Skipwith with a List of Books," 744; Witherspoon, *Lectures on Moral Philosophy*, 73–74, 97; Madison, "Letter to James Madison Sr.," 1:5. For a fuller discussion of Common Sense Realism on the American system, see Willis, *Inventing America*, esp. 175–77, 181–92, 237–38, and my *A Common Sense Theology*, 81–104.

25. Reid, *Essays on the Active Powers of Man*, 640, 595, 591, 589; Reid, *Practical Ethics*, 177. Reid was open to "tacit consent," which may be reflected in Article V of the Constitution.

26. Reid, *Essays on the Intellectual Powers of Man*, 365, 403, 437–38.

We have already noted some poll data suggesting that these commitments to descriptive meaning are not all dead in contemporary American society; American common-sense beliefs are still surviving. This entails that a theology articulating faith on these grounds might get a hearing.

The heritage of Common Sense Realism lives on in American pragmatism. One of the premier representatives of this philosophy, Richard Rorty, claims to be indebted to common-sense philosophy.[27] As a pragmatist, truth for him is related to practice and action,[28] that is, what works. In judging what is true, much to the surprise of many critics, he also endorses the possibility of achieving objective/descriptive truth. In dialogue with ontological constructions of reality he writes, "The point of edifying philosophy [ontology] is to keep the conversation going rather than to find objective truth, in the view I am advocating, is the result of normal discourse."[29] Normal discourse for Rorty is "that which is conducted with an agreed-upon set of conventions about what counts as a relevant contribution."[30] It is, he says, "any discourse (scientific, political, theological, or whatever) which embodies agreed-upon criteria for reaching agreement."[31] Note here that theology is identified by Rorty as normal discourse, and so on his grounds is capable of providing objective truth.

The point here seems to be that if we are to achieve objective, descriptive truth (including on such matters as descriptive normative meaning) we must first share certain formal presuppositions about how to reach agreement and what counts as a good argument. The theological model I have been developing operates with such formal presuppositions, we have noted. (See the suppositions about the kind of book the Bible is and the rules concerning the literal sense.) Consequently, on Rorty's grounds the Bible seems

27. Rorty, *Philosophy in the Mirror of Nature*, 142.

28. Rorty, *Consequences of Pragmatism*, 162.

29. Rorty, *Philosophy in the Mirror of Nature*, 377. For a similar interpretation of his thought, see J. Smith, *Who's Afraid of Relativism?*

30. Rorty, *Philosophy in the Mirror of Nature*, 320.

31. Rorty, *Philosophy in the Mirror of Nature*, 11.

capable of providing descriptive meaning over against experience, and so will not fall prey to Feuerbach's critique! Rorty's reflections also imply that the model of theology being developed here is also capable of offering objective truth. Certainly judgments about Christian truth can be made through careful study of the Bible's literal sense. But Rorty's insights might also be useful in thinking about how the model I offer can allow us to make extratextual truth claims through the "family resemblance" between Christian claims and scientific or historical realities. More on that in closing.

Another resource for the intelligibility of establishing the descriptive, normative meaning of biblical texts is science and the scientific method. Recall we have noted how scientists endorse objective meaning and truth when examining experimental data. In the lab, it does not matter if you are Black or white, male or female, straight or gay: water is comprised of hydrogen and oxygen; the heartbeat detected by one doctor can in principle be detected by another.[32] At least in one of the so-called "soft sciences," this overcoming of relativism is apparent, particularly in the anthropologist Clifford Geertz employed by Hans Frei in his efforts to explain the Bible's literal sense. He is concerned to offer "thick description," describing cultures not explaining them. This approach also seems open to the possibility of understanding cultures without necessarily empathizing with them.[33] Geertz's distinctions suggest the different phases of interpretation in Karl Barth's scheme, that when we agree that our aim is merely endeavoring to describe a reality we can offer a descriptive meaning. There seems to be a lot of intellectually respectable ways to challenge the relativism that runs rampant in Western society.

Speaking of objective meaning from a scientific perspective, neurobiological findings provide intriguing data to substantiate the possibility that we can read texts together without our distinct social contexts or personal experience dictating our agendas. It

32. For similar observations, see Boghossian, *Fear of Knowledge*, 110–11.

33. For Frei's use of Geertz, see Frei, *Types of Christian Theology*, 12–13, 26–27. For Geertz's approach, see his "From the Native's Point of View: On the Nature of Anthropological Understanding," 226.

seems that when we are reading texts our frontal and temporal lobes are active. There is debate about the role of the parietal lobe. Recent research, breaking with the earlier neurobiological consensus, finds that this lobe in the back of the brain has no role when we are engaged in reading activities. And even those contending for this part of the brain's role in reading activities note that it is the left parietal lobe that functions, not the superior parietal lobe that is responsible for body and spatial awareness.[34] In short, when we are reading, the parts of the brain that orient us in society and bring our personal experience or sense of self to phenomena or pages under analysis are minimized or shut down. It is not that we cannot in principle inject our social context and personal experience into discerning theological concepts, but these are distinct neural operations. Cutting-edge brain science reveals, then, that our brains are certainly capable of reading and discerning without injecting social context and into the discernment. There is scientific data to support the interpretive insights of New Criticism, Rorty, and Wittgenstein and their claim that descriptive interpretation of a text's objective meaning is possible.

It makes sense, then, for theology to seek to identify the literal sense of Scripture, merely to concentrate on *describing* the text's or the doctrine's meaning, even if in later stages of interpretation we move on to mediating or applying the text's or doctrine's significance for life today in our context. But these creative interpretations mingling the Word with our own experience/perspective are based on the objective, transcendent reality of the Word that stands over against us. In other words, it is one thing to be in love with an imaginary lover and another matter to be in love with a real live member of the opposite sex. In the first case, the lover's (alleged) existence is a product of one's needs and desires. But although in the second case the feelings of love inspired by the lover are reflections of one's experience and desires, this does not negate the reality of the actual existence of the lover, whose presence and hair color can be discerned objectively both by those who

34. Hickok and Poeppel, "The Cortical Organization of Speech Process"; Geschwind, "Disconnexion Syndromes in Animals and Man."

love him/her and those who do not. Why the theological community (indeed many of the humanities) has not availed itself of this Barthian distinction is an intriguing mystery, perhaps wrapped up in the mysteries of our sinful concupiscence. We all want to take credit for what we have put our distinct mark on. Maybe it's just as simple as that we have all been co-opted by the Kantian turn to the subject. But it has cost the church credibility in light of American and European culture's apparent co-option by the Feuerbachian critique of faith.

DISTORTING THE MEANING OF THE BIBLICAL TEXT: LESSONS TAUGHT BY THE THEORY OF UNCERTAINTY

In drawing on scientific insights to make the case for the possibility of discerning objective descriptive meaning, there is one other scientific insight relevant to the issue of meaning. I refer to the principle of uncertainty first developed by Werner Heisenberg in 1927. Its fundamental point is not to deny objective meaning but to make physicists more modest about what we can scientifically measure with certainty. It seems that, according to the principle, the more precisely a particle's position is known the less we know of its speed, and vice versa.[35] This entails that we cannot correctly identify both a particle's position and its speed.

There has been debate over whether this principle applies to macroscopic reality, to matter. And although it is true that the larger the object measured, the less calculating its location is affected by measuring its speed. But Heisenberg himself clearly believed that his finding does have applicability for how we understand the things of the world.[36] Let's take him at his word and apply the principle of uncertainty to reading the Bible.

We have noted that the prevailing paradigms that fall prey to Feuerbach's critique insist on a role for the interpreter's experience

35. Heisenberg, "Über den anschaulichen Inhalt der quartentheoretischen Kinematik und Mechanik."

36. Heisenberg, *The Physicist's Conception of Nature*, esp. 14–15, 25, 28–29.

in determining a text's meaning. They seem to be trying to establish both the biblical text's location (what it meant) and its motion (where it is going, what it means in our context or its movement from author's intention to final form). Heisenberg's principle entails that a focus on speed distorts your perception of the observed entity's location. In other words, it seems, when you are focused on motion (what a text entails for the future, including the present moment or focus on speculations about how the text came to be) you distort its location (what it originally meant)! By contrast, if you focus on its location (what it meant) without regard for its speed (where it might take us), like Barth claims happens in *explicatio*, you have a better chance of capturing its position (its original meaning). The guild of biblical scholars and theologians would do well to consider these logical, scientifically rooted points.

Speaking of the scientific method, its insights can also help us with another theological question, whether the meanings of and claim to Christian truth by the biblical text have any extra-textual referents, especially since on grounds of the theological proposal I have been articulating the Bible only makes literary, not historical or scientific claims. Postliberal theologians are often accused of being fideists. Let's see. We won't get far persuading the Nones and the rest of American society to consider Christianity very seriously if this allegation is true. But in fact, we can make the case that while only making literary claims, Christian faith's truth claims have a scientific character. That will get faith some attention in pop culture.

THE TRUTH OF CHRISTIANITY: SOME SCIENTIFIC, PRAGMATIC, AND HISTORICAL CONSIDERATIONS

The logical implications of the position I have been articulating seem to reflect commitments of postliberal theologian Hans Frei. I agree with him that the meaning of the biblical text is its truth, but only for the believer.[37] If you focus on the descriptive meaning of biblical texts then it seems you must agree with Frei that the concern is with what narrative means, never mind if it can be a life perspective for us.[38] How can the biblical text be true on such grounds?

The surprising answer is that the Bible can be true with this set of suppositions much like science can make truth claims. Recall that scientists themselves concede that science proceeds with certain formal suppositions/paradigms for assessing data. These paradigms guide the research and remain in place unless data emerge that contradict the paradigm and demand the need for the development of a new, more adequate paradigm.[39] But no less than the Christian commitment to the Bible, for the scientist there is no theory-independent view of reality. Theology, it seems, really is a science—the science of God. Even Karl Barth, who provides the basic framework for this chapter's proposal, claims that theology is a science in the sense of pursuing a distinct subject following a definite self-consistent path to knowledge, but not obliged to submit to claims of other sciences.[40]

Of course, the scientific method makes one other demand. Data must be repeatable, so that you can retest the results gained the first time.[41] It is interesting that historians operate this way as well. Late nineteenth/early twentieth-century liberal German scholar Ernst Troeltsch noted that historians operate with three principles, the third of which presupposes that for a reported event to be deemed historically verifiable it must have an analogy in present experience (the principle of analogy).[42] This has been a sticking point for Christians, as it in principle rules out most of the biblical miracles. There is no analogy in our present experience to

37. Frei, "Remarks in Connection with the Theological Proposal," 43.

38. Frei, "Remarks in Connection with the Theological Proposal," 40.

39. See nn. 1 and 36 above.

40. Barth, *Church Dogmatics*, I/1:7ff.

41. Giberson and Collins, *Language of Science and Faith*, 112; Polkinghorne, *Reason and Reality: The Relationship between Science and Theology*, 53.

42. Troeltsch, *Gesammelte Schriften*, 2:729–53; Troeltsch, "Historiography."

the resurrection, the feeding of the five thousand, changing water into wine, and perhaps even the healings. This is why most seminary graduates and other recipients of higher education are sure that these reports are not historical.

Yes, the disciplines and science and history share a common commitment. A phenomenon can only be scientific or historical if it is *repeatable*. That in principle rules out miracles, including creation and the incarnation of Jesus (as well as his resurrection). Yet at the same time there is the recognition that science cannot address everything. No less eminent scientists than Werner Heisenberg and Stephen Hawking made this claim.[43] We might ask historians why they do not display this sort of intellectual humility, and the failure of biblical scholars and church historians to acknowledge this is a big part of the problem theology has had since the Enlightenment.

Let's focus more on the mutual failure of science and history to explain everything. They can't explain the issues Christianity addresses. But this does not rule out that Christianity has scientific and historical implications. This accords with the previously noted idea of family resemblances between language-games (disciplines) introduced by Wittgenstein, an idea affirmed by Human Genome Project director Francis Collins.[44]

We can identify some points on which Christianity and science or history overlap. First Corinthians 15 mandates that Christians believe in a bodily resurrection of Jesus. Recall that the biblical narrative is tyrannical in authority. The biblical text takes control of readers and hearers; it resists our efforts to take control of its meaning and impose our meaning on it. As such, the narrative makes us forget ourselves and all the unhappiness and isolation experienced by a life wallowing in subjectivity. Instead, the biblical narrative draws us into its world so that we come to see

43. Heisenberg, *The Physicist's Conception of Nature*, 28; Hawking and Mlodinow, *The Grand Design*, 42; Giberson and Collins, *Language of Science and Faith*, 82.

44. See nn. 14 and 16 above. Also see Polkinghorne, *Reason and Reality*, 19.

ourselves as part of this world, come to interpret our own experience in light of the biblical and theological themes. Hans Frei more or less endorses this point. And George Lindbeck does as well.[45]

Frei also proceeds to note how Christ is portrayed in the Gospel narratives. The Jesus of the Gospel narratives has an unsubstitutable identity. He is depicted as "the resurrection and the life" (John 11:25). He is identified by one of the angels as the one who lives (Luke 24:5–7). Thus the Jesus rendered by the biblical accounts is one who is risen and lives. He cannot be known, then, by those who so submit to the accounts' tyrannical authority, only as Risen and alive.[46]

This entails that for Christians the affirmation of Jesus's resurrection must be factual—have a family resemblance to history. Why? Because in claiming as the church does that the only Jesus who exists is the one portrayed in the Gospels, if he is not risen, then the Christian version of Jesus would be false. Evidence, then, against Jesus's resurrection would count against the truth of Christianity. Paul essentially says this in 1 Corinthians 15:17.

To be sure, the church is not making an historical claim in the strict sense, but a Christian claim with factual implications. Historical evidence against the resurrection (and to date none exists) would count against Christianity's truth.

Is the resurrection an historical event? No. But it is not disproven, and so until or unless it is, we can call it a plausible fact (with a status not unlike the scientific claim that atoms exist, though they have not been seen, or the historic claims that there was a catastrophic flood in prehistoric times, that Oswald acted alone in killing Kennedy). It is plausible, and we might make the same claim about other biblical miracles and the exodus (whose historicity is currently under fire in the guild of biblical scholarship).[47]

---

45. Frei, *Eclipse of Biblical Narrative*, 1–3; Frei, *Types of Christian Theology*, 161; Lindbeck, *Nature of Doctrine*, 118.

46. Frei, *Identity of Jesus Christ*, 139–52. There is a kind of ontological proof character to this assertion; see Anselm, *Proslogion*, 2–3.

47. On the skepticism of the guild toward the historicity of the Exodus, see J. Collins, *The Bible after Babel*, 46.

On biblical grounds the truth of Christian faith would not be impacted were evidence produced that unequivocally challenged the facticity of the other biblical accounts or miracles. But if it were proven that the disciples stole Jesus's body, that he had not physically risen, the Christianity would be false. In its present status, as a plausible claim, can we say that Christianity and the resurrection have a status akin to the truths associated with atomic theory or string theory, which have not been proven? Of course, one might argue that these theories have more plausible evidence on their side.

Wait. Suppose we make the argument for Christianity's plausibility in a fashion more like another postliberal theologian, George Lindbeck, or as pragmatist Richard Rorty might. Lindbeck argues that as the Word of God absorbs our world, so it functions to constitute a form of life. On this basis he claims we can evaluate its truth (a very pragmatic kind of argument).[48] This way of arguing for Christian truth seems even more viable. Is it not plausible after studying the history of Western civilization and Eastern Europe to argue that Christianity has been very effective in nurturing the quality of life in these regions? Poll data also indicates that regular worshippers poll as happier than the general public, not just in the States but also in other nations like Germany and Mexico.[49] Is not such data strong enough to make plausible on grounds of the scientific method that Christianity is true? The theory does, after all, have supporting data and like any scientific theory is open to disproof. But it can only be disproven (breaking the paradigm employed) by data demonstrating that Christianity has not nurtured a good way of life for the faithful.[50]

---

48. Lindbeck, *Nature of Doctrine*, 118, 65.

49. Pew Research Center, "Religion's Relationship to Happiness, Civic Engagement and Health Around the World."

50. Skeptics might contend that such an argument only demonstrates the beneficial impact of religion on homo sapiens, not Christianity's truth. But we might address this by examining whether polls reveal that other religions nurture as much happiness as Christianity. Even if such data were not available, it would not preclude the plausibility of Christianity's truth. On religion being beneficial for homo sapiens, see Wade, *The Faith Instinct*, 54ff.; Bellah,

We might make the same case for affirming God's role in the development of the biblical text and its meaning. This hypothesis is related to making the case for how Christian truth can be affirmed or how useful the teachings of Christianity have been for homo sapiens. It seems reasonable to hypothesize that these teachings have been so salubrious because they are of God. Of course this is not scientifically verifiable. But divine inspiration of Scripture and the teachings of the church seem plausible on these grounds unless or until it is has been disproven.

SUMMARY REFLECTIONS

We have already indicated the respect for the authority of science and its findings on popular culture, how its claims are likely to get the attention of the Nones. Even today's relativists defer to science, giving it a privileged role in deciding factual questions. If you don't immediately agree with this observation of some cultural analysts, its veracity seems further illustrated in a statement by the Network of Spiritual Progressives on their website, as they appeal to science as the dialogue partner against which they feel they must justify network members' belief in spiritual experience.[51] Other examples of American veneration of science to this very date include a 2018 poll by Pew Research Center finding that of all the professions, scientists come in second, topped only by the military, on the question of whether the public has a great deal of trust in them.[52] Let us also not overlook the trust our educational establishment has put in the STEM formula. Science, Technology, Engineering, and Math are your most important subjects. The importance of science is the message our youth are receiving, a message that is more and more orienting their worldview.

Religion in Human Evolution.

51. For the website statement, see Mercadante, *Belief without Borders*, 4. For the overall analysis of our ethos, see Boghossian, *Fear of Knowledge*, 4; Deneen, *Why Liberalism Failed*, 13–16, 91–109; Wilson, *Conscilience*.

52. Pew Research Center, "Public Confidence in Scientists Has Remained Stable for Decades."

The theological approach I've proposed in this chapter cannot now readily be dismissed as just of interest to Christians, not in touch with cutting-edge academic developments. For those bold enough to remain open to the disproof of faith's miracles and its ability to nurture the good life, the truth-claims of Christianity can be presented as having the analogies to the force of a scientific theory! Polls of the Nones suggest that if this point is made along with the critique of the interpreter's role in determining the meaning of Christian beliefs it may have resonance with the religiously unaffiliated. In 2017 it was found that 60 percent of them questioned religious teachings and 34 percent did not like religious leaders.[53] Thus a version of Christianity that indicates a scientific credibility (not proof) for Christian claims might assist in addressing questions the Nones have. And leaving aside the opinions (interpretive input) of religious leaders in determining faith's meaning will not hurt faith's credibility.

There are other arguments that can be made on behalf of the viability of this model. We've noted how the theological model I've proposed for withstanding Feuerbach's critique in ensuring that Christianity cannot logically be reduced to human wish fulfillment links up with good old (American) common sense. Recall how the American republic was based on the philosophy of Scottish Common Sense Realism, which presupposes that we can "reason together." As such, a widespread hearing of a version of Christianity that posits the belief that truth can be discerned— is not relative—could help postmodern American society to get back to constitutional roots, to criticize the relativism and sense of irresponsibility (after all, our political ethos and media practices seem to suggest we are in a post-truth era) that has made inroads in society.

Even if you don't associate common sense with the philosophy of the American political system and its founders, the version of Christianity that I am presenting is common sense. As I have already noted, no matter how committed you are to relativism, to

53. Pew Research Center, "Why America's 'Nones' Don't Identify with a Religion."

the belief that we all have our own meanings, everyone living in nations with cars—gender, ethnicity, economic status, and sexual orientation aside—knows that when the light is red we should stop the car. And everyone who has read or even heard of Shakespeare's *Romeo and Juliet* knows it's a love story. The ability to read a book, like the narrative portions of the Bible, in a literal way, arriving at common descriptive meanings, is just common sense. When correctly explained, making clear that there is still space for unqiue individual reflections on and applications of Christianity's core teachings, the model of theology I am proposing can certainly communicate with ordinary people in our contexts, perhaps better than a theology advocating the deconstruction of biblical meaning or telling people to "construct" their own meanings.

Another consideration in establishing the viability of the post-Barthian model for theology I have proposed is to remember which theological heritages are best holding their own in a period of mainline church decline. Let's highlight again this model's endorsement of the narrative character of the Bible considered in its entirety and the belief that the authority of the biblical Word is tyrannical, overcoming our own world. These are commitments of the evangelical movement and the historic African-American tradition, with evangelicals insisting on biblical infallibility and the Black church with its "Bible-believing heritage."[54] And the polls indicate the success of these traditions in withstanding membership erosions and the growth of the Nones, as a 2018 Gallup poll finds that larger percentage of Blacks than whites (63 percent to 53 percent) are church members, and the decline in the last two decades is higher for whites than for African-Americans. While only 48 percent of white Protestants said that religion was very important

---

54. National Association of Evangelicals, "Statement of Faith." On Black church "Bible-believing," see Bentley, "Bible Believers in the Black Community," 110–11; Raboteau, *Slave Religion*, 311–13; T. Smith, *Conjuring Culture*, esp. 70–76, 250–54. The maintaining of this heritage is evident in a 2014 Pew Research Center poll, "Blacks More Likely than Others in U.S. to Read the Bible Regularly, See It as God's Word." Sixty-one percent of Black Protestants are likely to read the Bible weekly compared to 32 percent of whites, and 39 percent of Blacks deem the Bible God's Word compared to 22 percent of whites.

in 2018, 82 percent of evangelicals and Blacks made that claim, according to the Pew Research Center.[55] Correspondingly, an earlier Pew poll found that there is a disproportionately smaller number of African-Americans among the Nones, as African-Americans comprise 11 percent of the American population, but only 9 percent of the Nones are Black.[56]

Granted, all is not rosy for the Black church regarding African-American Millennials. One 2014 poll conducted by Youth Hope-Builders Academy revealed that 23.2 percent of Black Millennials qualify as Nones. This is certainly alarming, but it is a much lower figure than the 36 percent of unaffiliated Millennials, according to the most recent 2014 Pew Research Center report.[57]

The statistics make clear that a theological position committed to biblical authority and the literal meaning of the text is more likely to have significant success in our context than those opting for a position that falls prey to Feuerbach's critique of Christianity. And if you are inclined to dismiss this point on grounds that ethnic similarities (the Black church) and birth-rate (evangelicals have more kids than mainline Christians) account for these numbers, at least you have to admit that a theologically conservative commitment to biblical authority and the literal meaning of Scripture has not hurt these Christian streams, still work in our context. Can this insight, that theological positions not falling prey to Feuerbach's critique of Christianity, more concerned with the Bible's literal sense than with the latest relevant trend (as defined by white-collar professionals), still make a difference? Could it still matter? Let's see. It will depend on your reactions to the challenges issued in closing

55. Jones, "U.S. Church Membership Down Sharply"; Pew Research Center, "Demographics of Religiously Unaffiliated."

56. Pew Research Center, "The Unaffiliated."

57. Data reported in Wimberly, "Black Youth Speak Out," 106; Pew Research Center, "A Closer Look at America's Rapidly Growing Religious 'Nones.'"

Conclusion

Why It Could Still Matter

Can the insights of this book still matter? I'm ready to argue that they might change things if the mainline churches in Europe and the States really grappled with them. But if the main points (continue to) get ignored, expect more of what's been happening since the 1970s and previously. For as we've seen, the beginnings of mainline church decline in those years coincided with the demise of Neo-Orthodox impact on these churches, to be replaced by the hegemony of theologies guided by the latest cultural trends.

To reverse these developments, theological models rooted in the transcendent Word of God and its compelling authority will have the best chance to get noticed by our cultural gurus in order to grab the media's attention. For such theological commitments get religion out of the "private, subjectivist box" in which secularism places it. That's news!

This is also an approach more likely to be heard by a significant number of the Nones, for as we've noted most have not been raised in the church. Thus, many have never been confronted by the compelling authoritative Word, by the historical Christian faith, and its message of unconditional love, and so it may be a unique option for many of them. And besides, a significant number of the Nones (two-thirds according to a previously cited 2018 Pew Research Center poll) are at least open to spirituality and belief in God. And of course we'll need to present these models of Christianity in a more intellectually credible way than evangelicals have, sort of like I have in this book, in order to have a chance to get a hearing among the Nones and the cultural gurus.

I'm not naively optimistic. It is quite possible that the mainline denominations and the theological establishment will continue to dodge the issues raised in this book. But if the challenges I am issuing in this book get ignored, and if nothing gets better, then at least I will have the satisfaction that posterity might someday learn that this book had a formula for the church to correct matters and that perhaps the formula will still have validity even in the future.

Consequently, I want to close this book with some challenges to readers. My aim is to initiate a conversation that I've dreamed about for more than fifty years that the church and American (Western European) society might have. Willing to join me in this conversation?

Struggle with Feuerbach: make it clear that your theological position does not fall prey to his critique of Christianity. And if your position cannot avoid this critique, do something about it.

Note again my argument that Feuerbach's view of religion is in the air in popular culture. I've been trying to convince you that like him, many say religion is just a (human) crutch, something people lean on to get by. And so a theology that can't address Feuerbach's critique that religion is about human wants and wishes will be heard in pop culture as confirming what we knew about religion all along. You want to be sure that your way of doing theology, of talking about faith, does not fall prey to his contention that Christianity is ultimately nothing more than a human way of coping with our problems.

Maybe your theological position can overcome this critique. Maybe you think that you have the perfect middle ground between the Barthian-like postliberal fidelity to the Bible's literal meaning and still have a way of linking this fidelity to the Word with a role for the interpreter's contribution to determining its meaning. But share with me and other readers how you pull that off. If you can, please share the argument with us, so I (at least) can learn better how to do it. And if you can't get around Feuerbach's critique, but don't think it matters, share that argument with us too. Keep in mind that a dialogue with his idea that Christianity is essentially a human activity is a dialogue that those of us in academic circles need to carry on all the time with sociology, anthropology, psychology, and with Karl Marx. Let's really take Feuerbach's critique seriously in our writing and preaching for a while at least, just in case I'm right about how the neglect of his critique is the reason our mainline churches are in such a funk.

Don't get hung up on what I wrote about Feuerbach. In case I got him wrong (and I don't think I have), set me straight, but don't stop there. After setting me straight about him, still proceed to address the sociocultural dynamics I've raised and the challenges secularism poses for Christianity. Still be sure you can demonstrate how your theological perspective avoids reducing Christian affirmations to human experience and wish fulfillment. (Remember, just asserting you believe that God and grace transcend human experience makes no sense if your method entails that every theological assertion makes no sense in itself but must be connected to the creative contribution of the theologian.)

Mainline church leaders: keep in mind that when you are atheological, as is the way in most mainline church circles, that this challenge still refers to you. I am referring to those pastors and denominational leaders who in the name of being relevant and meeting people's needs lament that we not allow ourselves to be "trapped" or constrained by theology. When you don't do theology, because it's too academic, you are still doing theology, relying on a worldview or secular stories to orient yourself. And that worldview comes from human experience. In that case, whatever you say about faith that is prone to being reduced to human experience will fall prey to the Feuerbachian critique. Again, if I am wrong about this, write an article or just email me to prove my error on this point.

Mainline church leaders: get some programming that expressly addresses the growth of the Nones. Be sure

these new strategies don't fall prey to the Feuerba-chian critique.

We've noted the lack of these programs in the mainline denominations, at least the lack of programs that avoid the critique of Feuerbach. My challenge to denominational officers and to parish pastors is to try to do something about this crisis. Be careful to avoid the same old programs that have not been working. Instead of continuing to be preoccupied about packaging faith in "fresh," "relevant" ways (we've seen in this book how and why it hasn't worked too well), why not focus on biblical and theological literacy along with unstructured contacts with Nones? Worth a try? If not, share with us how your new programs are going to work in a detailed analysis, especially keeping in dialogue with Feuerbach's critique as a "devil's advocate" to what you plan to do. Above all, don't do nothing about this crisis, and don't do what you do in ways that perpetuate the sick theological model that's been dominating mainline church life since the 1960s and before.

Historical critics: practice some of the humility of scientists regarding what history can demonstrate and rule out.

This is just a reiteration of a point made in the previous chapter. Recall that scientists concede that there are issues that their discipline cannot address, and that they do not do a good job of dealing with unrepeatable events. Why should biblical critics not make these concessions and make them clear to students?[1] Be a little more humble about pronouncing which biblical accounts definitely did not happen.

Engage in discussions about whether Barth's theology or something like the proposal made in this book can address both Feuerbach's critique and our present cultural context. If not, don't just offer criticisms; share your alternative.

---

1. See pp. 102–103, nn. 41–43.

I am not so much concerned about your reactions to my own particular proposal, because the issues raised in this book are bigger than my theological position. Why not start with a famous option like Barth's? But any theological position with a method that prioritizes the transcendent Word of God over human experience affirms the tyrannical authority of the biblical Word, will do as a partner in conversation with Feuerbach. If the Barthian-like model you elect to consider falls short, be precise as to why. What would be a viable alternative that can address our present situation and why?

If you are still inclined to favor some correlation of the interpreter's perspective with God's Word, recall in the last chapter the poll indicating the Nones' suspicions of religious leaders. Why should they be drawn to a theology that posits an authoritative contribution of the church leader's/theologian's experience? And another poll undertaken by megachurch pastor and theologian James White indicated that the Nones believe in a "democracy of truth" like you receive in Wikipedia, in community.[2] Consequently, could a proposal like mine and Postliberal Theology, which finds the literal meaning of Christian symbols in Christianity's community consensus about them (tradition), and also is open to the disproof of Christianity by the consensus of the community of researchers (akin to how science functions), attract the attention of this segment of the population better than the theological alternatives that presently dominate in the academy and the church?

I reiterate that what I think most useful about this book is not necessarily my proposal, but to get church and academy talking about the Feuerbachian critique. That's why this book and its findings could matter. In that spirit, I point out that the model I have proposed is interdenominational—it will work for any Christian tradition and other theological schools willing to operate with the hermeneutical suppositions sketched. Barth's critique of natural theology and Lutheranism (he might have made it toward Eastern Orthodoxy and mysticism) with their characteristic stress on the intimate, essential relation of God and humanity, will not be privy

2. See p. 107, n. 53; White, *The Rise of the Nones*, esp. 58–61.

to his critique. For on grounds of the Barthian-like method this book proposes, even the claim that God has made himself intimately related to us is a claim that has objectivity and transcendence whose source is the divine Other, not a merely human claim aimed at elevating our worth—the Gnostic and Millennial claim that "I am god." There is a big difference between that claim and the modest contention that God has made us his beloved spouse, that his energy or intimate presence is in us. Barth's frets about these positions are unwarranted, as long as the biblical narrative is interpreted in its literal meaning (where the texts interpreted so warrant).[3]

What the proposal I have offered is endeavoring to do is what the French philosopher Albert Camus says we should, to rebel against our ethos. About those caught up in the ethos of pop culture and in the mainline church's way of thinking Camus's description of his day still fits ours: "For want of something better to do, they deified themselves."[4] Instead of acting like we are gods (what the Nones and most modern theologians are doing), we need to talk about and give an alternative. Of that alternative, Camus's advice is timely for Christians today. He would have us seek "to learn to live and to die, and, in order to be a man [woman], to refuse to be a god."[5] In other words, we live as servants of each other, empty of pretension and living only by grace (Rom 6:14; Col 3:1–7). A theology that nurtures a life lived this way will be content to take a back seat in interpretation, not to be so confident that he/she can manipulate texts to get them to meet our needs. Getting out of God's way, submitting to him and his Word, gives another effective testimony to God's transcendence, makes it clearer that faith is not about human experience. And then the testimony to and practice of God's *agape* (self-giving) love will be a little clearer.

3. For Barth's critique of mysticism, see *Church Dogmatics*, I/2:319ff.; II/1:10f. For his critique of natural theology, see *Church Dogmatics*, I/2:29ff.; II/1:85ff.

4. Camus, *The Rebel*, 305.

5. Camus, *The Rebel*, 306.

Don't think I'm as naive as this book title might suggest that I am. I am not suggesting that if we make church leaders aware of Feuerbach and widely disseminate theological positions like mine that can overcome his critique all will be well with European and American Christianity. Even if I am correct in my analyses in this book and my dreams were realized, the church (at least in America) will still need to do the sort of things that Rick Warren and other megachurch leaders learned from management consultant Peter Drucker—make gut-values connections, lead with authenticity and adaptability, engage in niche marketing, nurture a sense of community and small groups with authentic navigators. There will also be a need to develop a rich array of programs that are fun and enriching, perhaps those that target or give more responsibility to Millennials, as some researchers advise.[6] But the more we can get the theology I've been presenting embedded in the pulpits and denominational offices of our churches, the less you will need the kind of megachurch, successful business strategies we've been noting. Members caught up in the world of the Bible and Christian basics are usually your best, most engaged members and will loyally and joyfully serve without any gimmicks.

Even when we consider these qualifications, I still warn against naiveté. We are all wiser when reminded of a comment by postliberal theologian George Lindbeck, who has inspired my own proposal. As noted, he once observed a concern that the Word of God's role in shaping us, like this book advocates in order to counter Feuerbach's critique, faces an uphill battle in modernity because it impinges on a cherished achievement in modernity—our autonomy.[7]

Christianity in the West and our societies may be in the funk they're in because of our fixation on autonomy. Maybe in the next decades the church and society will not be ready for the alternative—to have our lives swallowed up by the tyrannical,

---

6. Drucker, "Management Paradigms"; cf. Sosnik et al., *Applebee's America*, esp. 93ff.; Wimberly, "Black Youth Speak Out," 117ff.; Schultz and Schultz, *Why Nobody Wants to Go to Church Anymore*.

7. Lindbeck, *The Nature of Doctrine*, 77.

grace-filled authority of God's portrait (narrative) of his plans for the cosmos. But when it transpires, Feuerbach's critique and our infatuation with things of the self will not have a chance. And then our churches might be revived from their funk. Let's continue the conversation about Feuerbach and the Nones. The health of our beloved Mother (the church) is at stake, but have no fear. God will still deliver her, and us.

Bibliography

Ahlstrom, Sydney E. *A Religious History of the American People.* New Haven: Yale University Press, 1974.

Alves, Rubem. *A Theology of Human Hope.* St. Meinrad, IN: Abbey, 1974.

Ammerman, Nancy. *Sacred Stories, Spiritual Tales: Finding Religion in Everday Life.* Oxford: Oxford University Press, 2013.

Anderson, Walter Truett. "Introduction: What's Going on Here?" In *The Truth about Truth: De-confusing and Re-constructing the Postmodern World,* edited by Walter Anderson, 1–11. New York: Tarcher, 1995.

Aslan, Reza. *God: A Human History.* New York: Random House, 2017.

Auerbach, Erich. *Mimesis: The Representation of Reality in Western Literature.* Translated by Willard Trask. Princeton: Princeton University Press, 1953.

Barna Research. "51% of Churchgoers Don't Know of the Great Commission." March 27, 2018. https://www.barna.com/research/half-churchgoers-not-heard-great-commission/.

———. "The End of Absolutes: America's New Moral Code." May 25, 2016. https://www.barna.com/research/the-end-of-absolutes-americas-new-moral-code/.

———. "Perception of Jesus, Christians & Evangelism in the UK." February 10, 2016. http:www.barna.com/research/perceptions-of-jesus-christians-evangelism-in-the-uk.

———. "What Do Americans Believe about Jesus? 5 Popular Beliefs." April 1, 2015. http:www.barna.com/research/what-do-americans-believe-about-jesus-5-popular-beliefs.

Barth, Karl. *Anselm: Fides Quaerens Intellectum; Anselm's Proof of the Existence of God in the Context of His Theological Scheme.* London: SCM, 1960.

———. *Church Dogmatics.* Edited by G. W. Bromiley and T. F. Torrance. 4 vols. Edinburgh: T. & T. Clark, 1936–62.

———. "An Introductory Essay." In Ludwig Feuerbach, *The Essence of Christianity,* translated by George Eliot, x–xxxii. New York: Harper & Row, 1957.

———. *Protestant Thought: From Rousseau to Ritschl.* Translated by Brian Cozens. New York: Simon & Schuster, 1969.

Bibliography

Bauerschmidt, Frederick C. "Aesthetics." In *Radical Orthodoxy*, edited by John Milbank et al., 201–19. London: Routledge, 1999.

Bellah, Robert. *Religion in Human Evolution*. Cambridge: Belknap Press of Harvard University Press, 2011.

Bentley, William H. "Bible Believers in the Black Community." In *The Evangelicals: What They Believe, Who They Are, Where They Are Changing*, edited by David F. Wells and John Woodbridge, 108–21. Nashville: Abingdon, 1975.

Berger, Peter. "Introduction." In *Between Relativism and Fundamentalism*, edited by Peter Berger, 1–13. Grand Rapids: Eerdmans, 2010.

———. *The Sacred Canopy: Elements of the Sociological Theory of Religion*. Garden City, NY: Doubleday, 1969.

Bloesch, Donald G. *A Theology of Word & Spirit: Authority & Method in Theology*. Downers Grove, IL: InterVarsity, 1992.

Bloom, Allan. *The Closing of the American Mind*. New York: Simon & Schuster, 1987.

Boghossian, Paul. *Fear of Knowledge: Against Relativism and Constructivism*. Oxford: Clarendon, 2006.

Braaten, Carl. *Because of Christ: Memoirs of a Lutheran Theologian*. Grand Rapids: Eerdmans, 2010.

Braaten, Carl, and Robert Jenson, eds. *Christian Dogmatics*. 2 vols. Philadelphia: Fortress, 1986.

Brenan, Megan. "Religion Considered Important to 72% of Americans." *Gallup News*, December 24, 2018. https://news.gallup.com/poll/245651/religion-considered-important-americans.aspx.

Brooks, Cleanth, and Robert Penn Warren. *Understanding Fiction*. New York: F. S. Crofts, 1944.

Brothers, Michael. *Distance in Preaching: Room to Speak, Space to Listen*. Grand Rapids: Eerdmans, 2014.

Brown, Robert MacAfee. "My Story and 'The Story.'" *Theology Today* 32 (1975) 166–73.

Brunner, Emil. *Offenbarung und Vernunft*. Zurich: Zwingli, 1941.

Bultmann, Rudolf. *Jesus Christ and Mythology*. New York: Scribner's, 1958.

Burton, Tara. *Strange Rites: New Religions for a Godless World*. New York: Hachette, 2020.

Buttrick, David. *Homiletic: Moves and Structures*. Philadelphia: Fortress, 1987.

Campbell, Charles L. *Preaching Jesus: The New Directions for Homiletics in Hans Frei's Postliberal Theology*. Grand Rapids: Eerdmans, 1997.

Camus, Albert. *The Rebel*. Translated by Anthony Bower. New York: Vintage, 1956.

Childs, Brevard. *Biblical Theology in Crisis*. Philadelphia: Westminster, 1970.

———. *Introduction to the Old Testament as Scripture*. Philadelphia: Westminster, 1979.

———. *The New Testament as Canon: An Introduction*. Philadelphia: Westminster, 1985.

Bibliography

Christian Reformed Church. *The Nature and Extent of Biblical Authority.* Grand Rapids: CRC, n.d.

Cobb, John, and David Griffin. *Process Theology.* Philadelphia: Westminster, 1976.

Collins, Francis. *The Language of God.* New York: Free Press, 2006.

Collins, John J. *The Bible after Babel: Historical Criticism in a Postmodern Age.* Grand Rapids: Eerdmans, 2005.

Cone, James. *Black Theology and Black Power.* New York: Harper & Row, 1969.

———. *A Black Theology of Liberation.* Maryknoll, NY: Orbis, 2010.

———. *God of the Oppressed.* Rev. ed. Maryknoll, NY: Orbis, 1997.

———. "The White Church and Black Power." In *Black Theology: A Documentary History, 1966–1979,* edited by Gayraud S. Wilmore and James Cone, 66–80. Maryknoll, NY: Orbis, 1979.

Cooper, Betsy, et al. *Exodus: Why Americans Are Leaving Religion—and Why They're Unlikely to Come Back.* Washington, DC: Public Religion Research Institute, 2016.

Copan, Paul. "Is God Just a Psychological Crutch for the Weak?" *Enrichment Journal* (2018).

Copeland, Kenneth. *Prosperity: The Choice Is Yours.* Fort Worth: Kenneth Copeland, 1985.

Cullmann, Oscar. *Christ and Time.* Translated by Floyd Filson. London: SCM, 1951.

Cumming, Richard. "Revelation as Apologetic Category: A Reconsideration of Karl Barth's Engagement with Ludwig Feuerbach's Critique of Religion." *Scottish Journal of Religion* 68 (2015) 43–60.

Daly, Mary. *Beyond God the Father.* Boston: Beacon, 1973.

Davidovich, Adina. *Religion as a Province of Meaning: The Kantian Foundations of Modern Theology.* Minneapolis: Augsburg Fortress, 1994.

Dehart, Paul J. *The Trial of the Witnesses: The Rise and Decline of Postliberal Theology.* Malden, MA: Blackwell, 2006.

De Jong, Allison. "Protestants Decline, More Have No Religion in a Sharply Shifting Religious Landscape (Poll)." *ABC News,* May 10, 2018. https://abcnews.go.com/Politics/protestants-decline-religion-sharply-shifting-religious-landscape-poll/story?id=54995663.

Deneen, Patrick J. *Why Liberalism Failed.* New Haven: Yale University Press, 2018.

Derrida, Jacques. *Limited Inc.* Edited by Gerald Graff. Evanston: Northwestern University Press, 1988.

———. *Of Grammatology.* Translated by Gayatri Chakravorty Spivak. Baltimore: Johns Hopkins University Press, 1970.

Dillenberger, John, and Claude Welch. *Protestant Christianity Interpreted through Its Development.* New York: Scribner's, 1954.

Dorrien, Gary. "The Future of Postliberal Theology." *The Christian Century,* July 18–25, 2001, 22–29.

———. *Kantian Reason and Hegelian Spirit.* Chichester, UK: Wiley, 2015.

Drucker, Peter. "Management Paradigms." *Forbes*, December 13, 2004.

Dunn, James D. G. *The New Perspective on Paul: Collected Essays*. Tübingen: Mohr/Siebeck, 2005.

Economist/YouGov. "Many Americans Are Scientific Skeptics." February 20, 2014. https://today.yougov.com/topics/politics/articles-reports/2014/02/20/many-americans-are-scientific-skeptics.

Ejxenbaum, B. M. "The Theory of the Formal Method." In *Readings in Russian Poetics: Formalist and Structuralist Views*, edited by Ladislav Matejka and Krystyna Pomorska. Cambridge: MIT Press, 1971.

Ellingsen, Mark. *A Common Sense Theology*. Macon, GA: Mercer University Press, 1995.

———. "The ELCA's Recent Decisions in Luther of Scientific Research." *Lutheran Forum*, October 2009. www.lutheranfurom.org/sexuality/the-elca2019s-recent-decisions-in-light-of-scientific-research.

———. *The Integrity of Biblical Narrative*. Philadelphia: Fortress, 1990.

———. "The Legacy of James Cone: How Do We Teach It For the 21st Century?" *Journal of the Interdenominational Theological Center* 47 (2019) 35–56.

———. *Martin Luther's Legacy: Reforming Reformation Theology for the 21st Century*. New York: Palgrave Macmillan, 2017.

Engels, Friedrich. *Ludwig Feuerbach and the Outcome of Classical German Philosophy*. Edited by C. P. Dutt. New York: International, 1941.

Evangelical Lutheran Church in America. "A Declaration of Our Inter-Religious Commitment." 2018. https://www.elca.org/Faith/. . .Inter-Religious. . ./Inter-Religious. . ./Draft-Policy-Statement.

———. "The Five Goals." 2019. http://www.elca.org/future.

Farley, Edward. *Ecclesial Man*. Philadelphia: Fortress, 1975.

Fetzer Institute. "Where We Belong: Mapping American Religious Innovation." 2015. https://fetzer.org/sites/default/files/images/resources/attachment/[current-date:tiny]/Where%20We%20Belong.pdf.

Feuerbach, Ludwig. *The Essence of Christianity*. Translated by George Eliot. New York: Harper & Row, 1957.

———. *Die Philosophie der Zukunft*. In H. Ehrenberg, *Frommanns Philosophische Taschenbücher*. Stuttgart: Leipzig, Quelle & Meyer, 1922.

———. *Thoughts On Death and Immortality*. Berkeley: University of California Press, 1980.

———. "Uber Spiritualismus und Materialismus, besonders in Beziehung auf die Willensfreiheit." In vol. 11 of *Gesammelte Werke*, edited by Werner Schuffenhauer. Berlin: Akademie, 1993.

———. *Das Wesen der Religion*. 1848/1851. Reprint, Berlin: Evangelische Verlagsanstalt, 2019.

Filson, Floyd. *The New Testament against Its Environment*. London: SCM, 1950.

Fiorenza, Francis Schüssler. "The Responses of Barth and Ritschl to Feuerbach." *Studies in Religion/Sciences Religieuses* 7 (1978) 160–65.

Bibliography

Frambach, Nathan. *Emerging Ministry: Being Church Today*. Minneapolis: Fortress, 2017.

Frank, Thomas. *Listen, Liberal: Or, What Ever Happened to the Party of the People?* New York: Holt, 2016.

Frei, Hans W. *The Eclipse of Biblical Narrative*. New Haven: Yale University Press, 1974.

————. *The Identity of Jesus Christ*. Philadelphia: Fortress, 1975.

————. "The 'Literal Reading' of Biblical Narrative in the Christian Tradition: Does It Stretch or Will It Break?" In *The Bible and the Narrative Tradition*, edited by Frank McConnell, 36–77. New York: Oxford University Press, 1986.

————. "Remarks in Connection with a Theological Proposal." In *Theology & Narrative: Selected Essays*, edited by George Hunsinger and William C. Placher, 26–44. New York: Oxford University Press, 1993.

————. "Response to 'Narrative Theology: An Evangelical Appraisal.'" *Trinity Journal* 8 (1987) 21–24.

————. "Theological Reflections on the Accounts of Jesus' Death and Resurrection." In *Theology & Narrative: Selected Essays*, edited by George Hunsinger and William Placher, 43–93. New York: Oxford University Press, 1993.

————. *Types of Christian Theology*. Edited by George Hunsinger and William C. Placher. New Haven: Yale University Press, 1992.

Geertz, Clifford. "'From the Native's Point of View': On the Nature of Anthropological Understanding." In *Interpretive Social Science*, edited by Paul Rabinow and William M. Sullivan. Berkeley: University of California Press, 1979.

Gerrish, Brian A. "Feuerbach's Religious Illusion." *The Christian Century*, April 9, 1997, 362–67.

Geschwind, Norman. "Disconnexion Syndromes in Animals and Man." *Brain* 88 (1965) 237–94.

Giberson, Karl W., and Francis S. Collins. *The Language of Science and Faith*. Downers Grove, IL: InterVarsity, 2011.

Glasse, John. "Barth on Feuerbach." *Harvard Theological Review* 57 (1964) 69–96.

Harkness, Georgia. *Understanding the Christian Faith*. New York: Abingdon-Cokesbury, 1947.

Hartford Institute of Religion Research. "Fast Facts about American Religion." hirr.hartsem.edu/research/fastfacts/fast_facts.html.

Harvey, Van A. *Feuerbach and the Interpretation of Religion*. Cambridge: Cambridge University Press, 1995.

————. *Feuerbach's Interpretation of Religion*. Cambridge: Cambridge University Press, 1997.

————. *The Historian and the Believer*. New York: Macmillan, 1966.

Hauerwas, Stanley. *A Community of Character*. Notre Dame: University of Notre Dame Press, 1986.

————. "Reframing Theological Ethics." In *The Hauerwas Reader*, edited by Michael Cartwright and John Berkman, 37–163. Durham: Duke University Press, 2001.

————. *With the Grain of the Universe: The Church's Witness against Natural Theology*. Grand Rapids: Baker, 2013.

Hauerwas, Stanley, et al. *Truthfulness and Tragedy: Further Investigations into Christian Ethics*. Notre Dame: University of Notre Dame Press, 1977.

Hawking, Stephen, and Leonard Mlodinow. *The Grand Design*. New York: Bantam, 2012.

Hegel, G. W. F. *Amplification of the Teleological Proof.* 1831.

————. *Lectures on the History of Philosophy.* 1805–6. Reprint, Lincoln, NE: University of Nebraska Press, 1995.

————. *Lectures on the Philosophy of Religion.* 1832. Reprint, Oxford: Oxford University Press, 2006.

————. *Lectures on the Proofs of The Existence of God.* 1830. Reprint, Oxford: Oxford University Press, 2007.

————. *Phenomenology of Spirit.* 1807. Reprint, Cambridge: Cambridge University Press, 2019.

————. *Preface to the Phenomenology of the Spirit.* 1807. Reprint, Princeton: Princeton University Press, 2005.

Heisenberg, Werner. *The Physicist's Conception of Nature*. Translated by Arnold J. Pomerans. London: Hutchinson, 1958.

————. "Über den anschaulichen Inhalt der quartentheoretischen Kinematik undMechanik." *Zeitschrift für Physik* 43 (1927) 173–98.

Henry, Carl F. H. *God, Revelation and Authority.* 6 vols. Waco, TX: Word, 1976–83.

Hickok, Greg, and David Poeppel. "The Cortical Organization of Speech Process." *National Review of Neuroscience* 8 (2007) 393–402.

Hodgson, Peter. *God in History: Shapes of Freedom*. Nashville: Abingdon, 1989.

Hodgson, Peter, and Robert King, eds. *Christian Theology: An Introduction to Its Traditions and Tasks*. Minneapolis: Fortress, 1985.

Howe, Reuel. *Man's Need and God's Action*. New York: Seabury, 1953.

Jakobson, Roman. "The Dominant." In *Readings in Russian Poetics: Formalist and Structuralist Views*, edited by Ladislav Matejka and Krystyna Pomorska. Cambridge: MIT Press, 1971.

————. "Poetry of Grammar and Grammar of Poetry." *Lingua* 21 (1968) 597–609.

Jefferson, Thomas. "Bill for Establishing Religious Freedom [in Virginia]." In *Writings*, 346–48. New York: Viking, 1984.

————. "Letter to Dugald Stewart." In *Writings*, 1487–89. New York: Viking, 1984.

————. "Letter to Robert Skipwith with a List of Books." In *Writings*, 740–45. New York: Viking, 1984.

Jenson, Robert. *Canon and Creed*. Louisville: Westminster John Knox, 2010.

Bibliography

Jones, Jeffrey M. "U.S. Church Membership Down Sharply in Past Two Decades." *Gallup News,* April 18, 2019. https://news.gallup.com/poll/248837/church-membership-down-sharply-past-two-decades.aspx.

Jones, Serene. *Feminist Theory and Christian Theology: Cartographies of Grace.* Minneapolis: Fortress, 2000.

———. "This God Which Is Not One: Irigaray and Barth on the Divine." In *Transfigurations: Theology and the French Feminists,* edited by C. W. Maggie Kim et al., 109–42. Minneapolis: Fortress, 1993.

Jones, Serene, and Paul Lakeland, eds. *Constructive Theology: A Contemporary Approach to Classical Themes.* Minneapolis: Augsburg Fortress, 2005.

Kant, Immanuel. *Critique of Pure Reason.* Translated by Norman Kemp Smith. Toronto: Macmillan, 1929.

Keller, Catherine, and Laurel Schneider, eds. *Polydoxy Theology.* New York: Routledge, 2011.

Knight, John Allan. *Liberalism versus Postliberalism: The Great Divide in Twentieth-Century Philosophy.* New York: Oxford University Press, 2013.

Kuhn, Thomas. *The Structure of Scientific Revolutions.* 2nd ed. New York: New American Library, 1970.

Lewis, John P. *Karl Barth in North America.* Eugene, OR: Resource, 2009.

LifeWay Research. "2018 State of American Theology Study: Research Report." http://lifewayresearch.com/wp-content/uploads/2018/10/Ligonier-State-of-Theology-2018-White-Paper.pdf.

Lindbeck, George. "The Church's Mission to a Postmodern Culture." In *Postmodern Theology: Christian Faith in a Pluralist World,* edited by Frederic Burnham, 37–55. San Francisco: Harper & Row, 1989.

———. *The Nature of Doctrine: Religion and Theology in a Postliberal Age.* Philadelphia: Westminster, 1984.

Lindberg, Carter. "Luther and Feuerbach." *Sixteenth Century Studies Journal* 1 (1970) 107–25.

Lonergan, Bernard. *Method in Theology.* London: Darton, Longman & Todd, 1971.

Luther, Martin. *Commentary on Galatians.* 1535. In *D. Martin Luthers Werke,* Kritische Gesamtausgabe (Weimarer Ausgabe), Vol. 40I. Weimar: Hermann Böhlaus Nachfolger, 1883ff.

———. *Confession Concerning Christ's Supper.* 1528. In *D. Martin Luthers Werke,* Kritische Gesamtausgabe (Weimarer Ausgabe), Vol. 26. Weimar: Hermann Böhlaus Nachfolger, 1883ff.

———. *The Eighteenth and Nineteenth Chapters of John.* 1528/29. In *D. Martin Luthers Werke,* Kritische Gesamtausgabe (Weimarer Ausgabe), Vol. 28. Weimar: Hermann Böhlaus Nachfolger, 1883ff.

———. *The Large Catechism.* 1529. In *The Book of Concord,* edited by Robert Kolb and Timothy J. Wengert, 377–480. Minneapolis: Fortress, 2000. And in *D. Martin Luthers Werke,* Kritische Gesamtausgabe (Weimarer Ausgabe), Vol. 30I. Weimar: Hermann Böhlaus Nachfolger, 1883ff.

Bibliography

———. *Lectures on Romans.* 1515/1516. In *D. Martin Luthers Werke*, Kritische Gesamtausgabe (Weimarer Ausgabe), Vol. 56. Weimar: Hermann Böhlaus Nachfolger, 1883ff.

Madison, James. "Letter to James Madison Sr." In *The Complete Madison: His Basic Writings*, vol. 1, edited by Saul Padover. New York: Harper, 1953.

Marx, Karl. "Contribution to the Critique of Hegel's Philosophy of Law: Introduction (1844)." In *Marx and Engels Collected Works*. 50 vols. Moscow: Progress, 1931.

———. "Contribution to the Critique of Hegel's Philosophy of Right." In *Karl Marx: Early Writings*, edited by T. B. Bottomore, 43–59. New York: McGraw-Hill, 1964.

———. "Theses on Feuerbach." In Frederick Engels, *Ludwig Feuerbach and the Outcome of Classical German Philosophy*. New York: International, 1941.

Mbiti, John. "The Encounter of Christian Faith and African Religion." *Christian Century*, August 27–September 3, 1980, 817–20.

McCormack, Bruce L., and Clifford B. Anderson, eds. *Karl Barth and American Evangelicalism*. Grand Rapids: Eerdmans, 2011.

McGill, Jenny. "An Interview with Alister McGrath." *DTS Magazine*, December 1, 2012, https://voice.dts.edu/article/an-interviewwith-alister-mcgraith-mcgill-junny/.

McGrath, Alister. *Bridge-Building: Effective Christian Apologetics*. Downers Grove, IL: InterVarsity, 1992.

———. *A Scientific Theology.* Vol. 2, *Reality*. London: T. & T. Clark, 2006.

Mercadante, Lisa. *Belief without Borders: Inside the Minds of the Spiritual but Not Religious*. New York: Oxford University Press, 2014.

Moltmann, Jürgen. *Theology of Hope*. Translated by James Leitch. New York: Harper & Row, 1976.

Murray, Charles. *Coming Apart: The State of White America, 1960–2010*. New York: Cox and Murray, 2012.

National Association of Evangelicals. "Statement of Faith." 1942. https://www.nae.net/statement-of-faith/.

Nelson, E. Clifford et al., eds. *The Lutherans in North America*. Philadelphia: Fortress, 1975.

Neuhaus, Richard John. "Presbyterians: Where Have All the People Gone?" *First Things*, December 1992, 66–68.

"New Harvard Research Says U.S. Christianity Is Not Shrinking, but Growing Stronger." *The Federalist*, January 22, 2018. https://thefederalist.com/2018/01/22/new-harvard-research-says-u-s-christianity-not-shrinking-growing-stronger/.

Newport, Frank. "Americans' Confidence in Institutions Edges Up." *Gallup News*, June 26, 2017. https://news.gallup.com/poll/212840/americans-confidence-institutions-edges.aspx.

———. "Near Record High See Religion Losing Influence in America." *Gallup News*, December 29, 2010. https://news.gallup.com/poll/145409/near-record-high-religion-losing-influence-america.aspx.

Nietzsche, Friedrich. *Thus Spoke Zarathustra*. 1892. Reprint, Oxford: Oxford University Press, 2009.

Nonprofits Source. "Church and Religion, Charitable Giving Statistics." 2019. https://nonprofitssource.com/online-giving-statistics/church-giving/.

Oden, Thomas. *A Change of Heart*. Downers Grove, IL: InterVarsity, 2014.

Osteen, Joel. *Your Best Life Now*. New York: Faith Words, 2004.

Pala, Luis. *God Is Relevant*. New York: Galilee Doubleday, 1997.

Pannnenberg, Wolfhart. *Jesus—God and Man*. Translated by Lewis L. Wilkins and Duane A. Priebe. 2nd ed. Philadelphia: Westminster, 1977.

Pembroke, Neil. *Divine Therapeia and the Sermon: Theocentric Therapeutic Preaching*. Eugene, OR: Pickwick, 2013.

Pew Research Center. "19 Striking Findings from 2019." December 13, 2019. https://www.pewresearch.org/fact-tank/2019/12/13/19-striking-findings-from-2019/.

———. "5 Facts about Religion in Canada." July 1, 2019. https://www.pewresearch.org/fact-tank/2019/07/01/5-facts-about-religion-in-canada/.

———. "Americans Have Positive Views about Religion's Role in Society, but Want It out of Politics." November 15, 2019. https://www.pewforum.org/2019/11/15/americans-have-positive-views-about-religions-role-in-society-but-want-it-out-of-politics/.

———. "America's Changing Religious Landscape." May 12, 2015. https://www.pewforum.org/2015/05/12/americas-changing-religious-landscape/.

———. "Blacks More Likely than Others in U.S. to Read the Bible Regularly, See It as God's Word." May 7, 2018. https://www.pewresearch.org/fact-tank/2018/05/07/blacks-more-likely-than-others-in-u-s-to-read-the-bible-regularly-see-it-as-gods-word/.

———. "Canada's Changing Religious Landscape." June 27, 2013. https://www.pewforum.org/2013/06/27/canadas-changing-religious-landscape/.

———. "A Closer Look at America's Rapidly Growing Religious 'Nones.'" May 13, 2015. https://www.pewresearch.org/fact-tank/2015/05/13/a-closer-look-at-americas-rapidly-growing-religious-nones/.

———. "Demographics." October 9, 2012. https://www.pewforum.org/2012/10/09/nones-on-the-rise-demographics/.

———. "Demographics of Religiously Unaffiliated." March 21, 2019. https://www.pew.forum.org/2012/10/09/nones-on-the-rise-demographics/.

———. "Educational Attainment among the Religiously Unaffiliated." December 13, 2016. https://www.pewforum.org/2016/12/13/educational-attainment-among-the-religiously-unaffiliated/.

———. Global Attitudes Project. Spring 2011. https://www.pewresearch.org/global/datasets/.

———. "How Does Pew Research Center Measure the Religious Composition of the U.S? Answers to Frequently Asked Questions." July 5, 2018. https://www.pewforum.org/2018/07/05/how-does-pew-research-center-measure-the-religious-composition-of-the-u-s-answers-to-frequently-asked-questions/.

———. "How Religious Commitment Varies by Country among People of All Ages." June 13, 2018. https://www.pewforum.org/2018/06/13/how-religious-commitment-varies-by-country-among-people-of-all-ages/.

———. "Importance of Religion and Religious Beliefs." November 3, 2015. https://www.pewforum.org/2015/11/03/chapter-1-importance-of-religion-and-religious-beliefs/.

———. "In U.S., Decline of Christianity Continues at Rapid Pace." October 17, 2019. https://www.pewforum.org/2019/10/17/in-u-s-decline-of-christianity-continues-at-rapid-pace/.

———. "Most U.S. Teens See Anxiety and Depression as a Major Problem Among Their Peers." February 20, 2019. https://www.pewsocialtrends.org/2019/02 /20/most-u-s-teens-see-anxiety-and-depression-as-a-major-problem.

———. "Public Confidence in Scientists Has Remained Stable for Decades." March 22, 2019. https://www.pewresearch.org/fact-tank/2019/03/22/public-confidence-in-scientists-has-remained-stable-for-decades/.

———. "Religion's Relationship to Happiness, Civic Engagement and Health Around the World." January 31, 2019. https://www.pewforum.org/2019/01/31/religions-relationship-to-happiness-civic-engagement-and-health-around-the-world/.

———. "The Unaffiliated." 2014. https://www.pewforum.org/religious-landscape-study/religious-tradition/unaffiliated-religious-nones/.

———. "When Americans Say They Believe in God, What Do They Mean?" August 26, 2018. https://www.pewforum.org/2018/04/25/when-americans-say-they-believe-in-god-what-do-they-mean/.

———. "Why America's 'Nones' Don't' Identify with a Religion." August 8, 2018. https://www.pewresearch.org/fact-tank/2018/08/08/why-americas-nones-dont-identify-with-a-religion/.

———. "Young Adults around the World Are Less Religious." June 13, 2018. https://www.pewforum.org/2018/06/13/young-adults-around-the-world-are-less-religious-by-several-measures/.

Polkinghorne, John. *Reason and Reality: The Relationship between Science and Theology*. Philadelphia: Trinity, 1991.

Public Religion Research Institute and Religion News Service. *Exodus: Why Americans are Leaving Religion*. August 2016. https://www.prri.org/wp-content/uploads/2016/09/PRRI-RNS-Unaffiliated-Report.pdf.

Punt, Jeremy. "Postcolonial Biblical Criticism in South Africa: Some Mind and Road Mapping." *Neotestamentica* 37 (2003) 59–85.

Raboteau, Albert J. *Slave Religion: The "Invisible Institution" in the Antebellum South*. Oxford: Oxford University Press, 2004.

Rad, Gerhard von. *Old Testament Theology*. Translated by D. M. G. Stalker. 2 vols. New York: Harper & Row, 1962–65.

Bibliography

Rahner, Karl. *Theological Investigations*. Vol. 9. Translated by Graham Harrison. London: Darton, Longman & Todd, 1972.

Ray, Stephen G., Jr., and Laurel Schneider, eds. *Awake to the Moment: An Introduction to Theology*. Louisville: Westminster John Knox, 2016.

Reid, Thomas. *Essays on the Active Powers of Man*. In *The Works of Thomas Reid, D.D.*, edited by William Hamilton. 7th ed. Edinburgh: Maclachlon and Stewart, 1872.

———. *Essays on the Intellectual Powers of Man*. Edited by A. D. Woozley. London: Macmillan, 1941.

———. *Practical Ethics*. Edited by Knud Haakonssen. Princeton: Princeton University Press, 1990.

"Religion." *Gallup News*. https://news.gallup.com/poll/1690/religion.aspx. 2018.

Religion News Service and *The Christian Century*. "Number of Nones Equals Evangelicals, Catholics." April 4, 2019. https://www.christiancentury.org/article/news/number-nones-equals-evangelicals-catholics.

Richards, I. A. *Practical Criticism*. London: Kegan, Paul, Trench, Trubner, 1930.

———. *Principles of Literary Criticism*. New York: Harcourt, Brace & World, 1925.

Ricoeur, Paul. *Essays on Biblical Interpretation*. Edited by Lewis S. Mudge. Philadelphia: Fortress, 1980.

———. *Interpretation Theory: Discourse and the Surplus of Meaning*. Fort Worth: Texas Christian University Press, 1976.

———. *Time and Narrative*. Translated by Kathleen McLaughlin and David Pellauer. 3 vols. Chicago: University of Chicago Press, 1983–88.

Ronsvalle, John, and Sylvia Ronsvale. *The State of Church Giving through 2011*. Champaign, IL: Empty Tomb, 2013.

Rorty, Richard. *Consequences of Pragmatism*. Minneapolis: University of Minnesota Press, 1982.

———. *Philosophy in the Mirror of Nature*. Princeton: Princeton University Press, 1979.

Rose, Matthew. "Karl Barth's Failure." *First Things*, June 2014. https://www.firstthings.com/article/2014/06/karl-barths-failure.

Ruether, Rosemary R. *Sexism and God-Talk: Towards a Feminist Theology*. Boston: Beacon, 1983.

Saad, Lydia. "Three in Four in U.S. Still See the Bible as Word of God." *Gallup News*, June 4, 2014. https://news.gallup.com/poll/170834/three-four-bible-word-god.aspx.

Schaeffer, Francis. *The God Who Is There*. Downers Grove, IL: InterVarsity, 1968.

Schillebeeckx, Edward. *Jesus: An Experiment in Christology*. Translated by Hubert Hoskins. New York: Crossroad, 1981.

Schleiermacher, Friedrich. *Christian Faith*. Edited by H. R. Mackintosh and J. S. Stewart. New York: Harper & Row, 1963.

Bibliography

Schmemann, Alexnader. "Worship in a Secular Age." In *An Eerdmans Reader in Contemporary Political Theology*, edited by William T. Cavanaugh et al., 105–18. Grand Rapids: Eerdmans, 2012.

Schultz, Thom, and Joani Schultz. *Why Nobody Wants to Go to Church Anymore.* Loveland, CO: Group Publishing, 2013.

Sennett, Richard. *The Corrosion of Character: The Personal Consequences of Work in the New Capitalism.* New York: Norton, 1998.

Sherwood, Harriet. "More than Half UK Population Has No Religion, Survey Finds." *The Guardian*, September 4, 2017. https://www.theguardian.com/world/2017/sep/04/half-uk-population-has-no-religion-british-social-attitudes-survey.

Smith, James K. A. *How (Not) to Be Secular.* Grand Rapids: Eerdmans, 2014.

———. *Who's Afraid of Relativism?* Grand Rapids: Baker, 2014.

Smith, Oliver. "Mapped: The World's Most (and Least) Religious Countries." *The Telegraph*, January 14, 2018.

Smith, Theophus H. *Conjuring Culture: Biblical Formations of Black America.* Oxford: Oxford University Press, 1994.

Sosnick, Douglas B., et al. *Applebee's America: How Successful Political, Business, and Religious Leaders Connect with the New American Community.* New York: Simon & Schuster, 2006.

Sri, Edward. *Who Am I to Judge?* San Francisco: Ignatius, 2016.

Statista. "Church Attendance of Americans 2019." https://www.statista.com/statistics/245491/church-attendance-of-americans/#statisticContainer.

Strauss, D. F. *Life of Jesus, Critically Examined.* Translated by Marian Evans. New York: Blanchard, 1855.

Syrotinski, Michael. *Deconstruction and the Postcolonial: At the Limits of Theory.* Liverpool: Liverpool University Press, 2007.

Taylor, Charles. *A Secular Age.* Cambridge: Harvard University Press, 2007.

Taylor, Mark C. "Discrediting God." *Journal of the American Academy of Religion* 62 (1994) 603–23.

Tillich, Paul. *Systematic Theology.* Chicago: University of Chicago Press, 1971.

Tracy, David. *Blessed Rage for Order.* New York: Seabury, 1978.

———. *Plurality and Ambiguity.* San Francisco: Harper & Row, 1987.

Troeltsch, Ernst. *Gesammelte Schriften.* 4 vols. Edited by Hans Baron. Tübingen: Mohr, 1912–25.

———. "Historiography." In *Encyclopedia of Religion and Ethics*, edited by James Hastings, vol. 6, 718–23. New York: Scribner's, 1914.

Turner, James. *Without God, Without Creed: The Origins of Unbelief in America.* Baltimore: John Hopkins University Press, 1985.

Twenge, Jean. *Generation Me.* New York: Free Press, 2006.

———. *iGen: Why Today's Super-Connected Kids Are Growing Up Less Rebellious, More Tolerant, Less Happy—and Completely Unprepared for Adulthood.* New York: Simon & Schuster, 2017.

Vanhoozer, Kevin. *Remythologizing Theology: Divine Action, Passion, and Authorship.* New York: Cambridge University Press, 2010.

Bibliography

Vanhoozer, Kevin, and Daniel Treier. *Theology and the Mirror of Scripture.* Downers Grove, IL: InterVarsity, 2015.

Van Til, Cornelius. *The New Modernism: An Appraisal of Barth and Brunner.* London: James Clarke, 1946.

Vogel, Manfred. "The Barth-Feuerbach Confrontation." *Harvard Theological Review* 59 (1966) 27–52.

Wade, Nicholas. *The Faith Instinct: How Religion Evolved & Why It Endures.* New York: Penguin, 2009.

Ware, Frederick. *Methodologies of Black Theology.* Cleveland: Pilgrim, 2002.

Weber, Joseph C. "Feuerbach, Barth, and Theological Methodology." *The Journal of Religion* 46 (1962) 24–36.

Wellhausen, Julius. *Prolegomena zur Geschichte Israels.* Berlin: Reimer, 1883.

White, James E. *The Rise of the Nones: Understanding and Reaching the Religiously Unaffiliated.* Grand Rapids: Baker, 2014.

Willis, Gary. *Inventing America: Jefferson's Declaration of Independence.* New York: Vintage, 1979.

Wilson, Edward O. *Conscilience: The Unity of Knowledge.* New York: Knopf, 1998.

Wimberly, Anne Streaty. "Black Youth Speak Out: An Urgent Call for Hope-Bearing Response." *Journal of Pastoral Theology* 26 (2016) 102–20.

Wimsatt, William K. *The Verbal Icon.* London: Methuen, 1954.

Wimsatt, William K., and Cleanth Brooks. *Literary Criticism: A Short History.* 2 vols. Chicago: University of Chicago Press, 1957.

Winseman, Albert L. "U.S. Church Looking for a Few White Men." July 27, 2004. https://news.gallup.com/poll/12463/us-churches-looking-few-white-men.aspx.

Wise, Carroll A. *The Meaning of Pastoral Care.* New York: Harper & Row, 1966.

Witherspoon, John. *Lectures on Moral Philosophy.* Edited by Jack Scott. Newark: University of Delaware Press, 1982.

Wittgenstein, Ludwig. *Philosophical Investigations.* Translated by G. E. M. Anscombe. 3rd ed. New York: Macmillan, 1958.

Wolfe, Alan. *Moral Freedom: The Search for Virtue in a World of Choice.* New York: Norton, 2001.

Wright, G. Ernest. *God Who Acts.* London: SCM, 1964.

Wright, N. T. *What Saint Paul Really Said: Was Paul of Tarsus the Real Founder of Christianity?* Grand Rapids: Eerdmans, 1997.

Wuthnow, Robert. *The Restructuring of American Religion: Society and Faith since World War II.* Princeton: Princeton University Press 1988.

Wyman, Jason A. *Constructing Constructive Theology: An Introductory Sketch.* Minneapolis: Fortress, 2017.

Index

Index

Index

CPSIA information can be obtained
at www.ICGtesting.com
Printed in the USA
FSHW010811130221
78550FS